THE NEGRO CHARACTER IN
AMERICAN LITERATURE

The Negro Character in American Literature

BY

JOHN HERBERT NELSON

AMS PRESS
NEW YORK

Reprinted from the edition of 1926, Lawrence
First AMS EDITION published 1970
Manufactured in the United States of America

International Standard Book Number: 0-404-00203-X

Library of Congress Card Catalog Number: 73-128982

AMS PRESS, INC.
NEW YORK, N.Y. 10003

PREFATORY NOTE

Several years ago, in looking about for a thesis subject which would be worth investigating in itself and at the same time lead to a survey of the whole field of American literature, I was attracted to certain American fictional types, particularly to the negro—perhaps the best portrayed of them all. His literary history seemed worth recording, partly because he arrived at his present estate only after a long and interesting journey, and partly because it would, incidentally, throw much light on our native drama, balladry, and fiction. Accordingly, I chose the subject; and the result stands substantially embodied in the following study, originally a dissertation submitted for the doctorate at Cornell University, in September, 1923. Most of the chapters have been condensed, the whole has been rewritten and reorganized, and a bibliography (which would now include more than twelve hundred titles) and an appendix on negro dialect have been omitted.

It is with pleasure that I acknowledge here my obligations to several friends and colleagues: Professor M. W. Sampson, Professor J. Q. Adams, and Professor William Strunk, of Cornell University; Professor G. D. Sanders, of the University of Arizona; Professor S. L. Whitcomb, Professor F. H. Hodder, and Professor W. S. Johnson, of the University of Kansas. Dr. Walter H. French, of Cornell, has offered many pertinent criticisms of the manuscript; and Professor F. C. Prescott, of Cornell, under whose guidance the work was originally prosecuted, has from the beginning been both helpful and encouraging.

J. H. N.

Lawrence, Kansas
  Sept. 25, 1926

CONTENTS

The Negro Character in American Literature

CHAPTER I

INTRODUCTION

The negro has been known to literature for many ages and in many lands. Homer's age knew him, as well as our own. Among the earliest Egyptian inscriptions are records of a black race which dwelt beyond the headwaters of the Nile. The ancient Greeks, the Romans, the Arabs, the Persians, the Spaniards, the French, the Germans, the English-speaking nations have all made the negro, in one way or another, a theme in song and story. Most of all, however, he has come to be associated with the New World, in particular with the United States. Here, where for so long he labored in bondage and where has subsequently come his greatest opportunity for development and cultural growth, he has ever been an important and unsolved problem for society, and in recent decades, at least, a human type highly attractive to writers of fiction. Neither sociologists nor novelists could afford to neglect him if they would.

The ancient world called him an Ethiopian, and at times confused him with the Arab; but that this ancient world knew his actual physical appearance is proved beyond dispute by Herodotus's well known description, as well as by extant sketches illustrating the myth of the pygmies and the cranes. The Greeks had much to say about the African. Homer sang of Memnon, Prince of the Ethiopians; Cepheus and his daughter Andromeda were Ethiopians; and if a somewhat fanatical German student of the subject be correct (which seems unlikely), Agamemnon himself belonged to a race having kinky hair.[1] Pindar, Euripides, Hippocrates, Plutarch, Lucian, and Diogenes Laertius all mention the African. To these might be added another list, of distinguished Roman names; for the Latin authors followed their Greek masters in this, as in most else, so that in many an historical passage or poem of theirs, we find references to the Ethiopian across the Mediterranean.

---

[1] See Christian Belger: *Die mykenische Lokalsage von den Gräbern Agamemnons und der seinen im Zusammenhange der griechischen Sagenentwickelung* [a dissertation], Berlin, 1893.

Again, in the Bible, or rather in rabbinical commentary on the Scriptures, certain scholars find evidence that the wife of Moses and the Queen of Sheba were Ethiopians; and in addition, there is the trite explanation (also from rabbinical lore) of the origin of the black race through Ham. It should perhaps be expected that the folk-literature of the Arabs, a migratory people who early crossed the Sahara and met the black man in his native haunts, should deal frequently with the negro. *The Arabian Nights* abounds in blackamoors—minor characters, who appear repeatedly as slaves to royalty or as paramours to highborn ladies. In spite of these early mentions, however, there was no adequate presentation of the black man in the literature of Greece, Rome, or the Oriental nations. He was no more than a name; his characteristics, his outlook on life, his ancestral heritage, so far as any of these were indicated, differed not at all from those of the Greek, or, more accurately, from those of common man.

Nor was there any more accurate presentation during the Middle Ages; on the contrary, there was none at all. Medieval Europe was in no condition to foster artistic productions, except as they pertained to the Church. Overrun by barbarian hordes, thrown into social and political chaos, she suffered a hectic existence for some centuries, only to become in time priest-ridden and oppressed by feudal chieftains. Culture and learning existed only in isolated spots; the drama and the historical writings of the ancient world were practically forgotten; and far from taking an interest in humanity as humanity, the few writers who throve at all regarded men principally as theological problems. Africa was known only as a dread region to the south, where lived the terrible Mohammedan; and as for the negro, his existence was scarcely remembered or known. True, the age sometimes thought of black men, but these fellows were devils, begrimed with the smoke and flame of everlasting fires, come up from Hell to tempt the chosen of Christ.[2] Such demons more aptly typified the interest of the period than could have any mortal being.

With the Renaissance, however, there came a change. Europe reawakened to an interest in things secular. Latin gave way to

---

[2] See the *Exempla* of Jacques de Vitry and *Dialogus Miraculorum* of Cæsarius von Heisterbach. Occasional black men also strayed into the romances of chivalry; *The Mabinogion,* for example, contains several such.

numerous vernaculars; nations slowly formed themselves out of the
disjointed domain of the Holy Roman Empire; new lands were ex-
plored, new peoples discovered or rediscovered; medieval religious
drama was replaced by another purely secular; literature began
once more to flourish.   In this newly arisen literature very early
appeared the negro, first in Spain and afterwards in other countries.
To understand how he came there, and how he was thus reintroduced to Europe, it is necessary to look briefly at Spanish history.

In the year 711, there crossed into Spain from Morocco the
Berber general Tarik, invited hither by conspirators against the
Visigoth king.   Overcoming this king easily, and finding little opposition ahead, Tarik marched inland, and, aided by Musa, his over-
lord in northern Africa, conquered the whole land, as far as the
foot of the Pyrenees.   Thus began a period of Moorish rule which,
with periodic interruptions, lasted more than five centuries, and
which Spain was able to throw off entirely only after Castile and
Aragon joined forces, upon the marriage of Ferdinand and Isa-
bella.   During the whole period the invaders marched throughout
the land, and to all Spaniards became a familiar sight—dark-skinned,
fierce-looking horsemen, in whose train followed still more dark
and fierce-looking men, mercenary negro troops from beyond the
Niger.   All of the intruders—Arab, Berber, Syrian, negro alike—
came to be regarded as hereditary enemies of the Spaniard,
and collectively they were called by the name "Moor," without
much regard for their wide racial differences.   The term remained,
and with it some confusion: Moor and the true negro were con-
founded, and this confusion was to last for centuries and pass into
other lands.   Many of the Moors, especially of the lower class,
settled in the land, where some remained even after the fall of
Grenada.   Spanish writers, therefore, early found in the Moor a
literary theme, first as a fierce enemy, and later as a foreign servant
type suitable for drama and certain kinds of fiction.   Nothing was
more natural than to use such a subject, and this use was early made
—from the very beginning of Spanish literature, in fact.   Spanish
epic poems of the twelfth century and following, notably the *Poema
del Cid,* treat of the struggle against the Mohammedan conquerors,
and in them the Moor is of course the villain of the story, the an-
tagonist of the heroic Spaniards.   Popular balladry, which seems
now to have followed the epics, continued the theme, with the

Moor viewed in the same light. Next he was adopted by the romancers and semi-historical chroniclers, who, for the most part, flourished after the danger from Mohammedanism had passed, and who thus were less severe in portrayal. And finally, the Moor made his appearance in the drama and the picaresque novel. A troop of Moorish characters appeared after the uprising of 1569, which was promptly treated in play after play. Throughout the sixteenth century, Spanish farces frequently employ African characters;[3] and in the very first of the picaresque novels, *Lazarillo de Tormes* (1554), a rascally Moorish servant contributes much to the interest of the story. In none of these works, however, nor in the epics, ballads, and historical chronicles which had preceded them, does the Moor appear, strictly speaking, negroid. In the earlier literature he was the fierce and swarthy enemy of Spain; in the later writings he is usually a servant type, at times comical, more often merely objectionable or else a puppet. Nevertheless, in the person of this composite and conventionalized foreigner, Spain reintroduced the negro to Europe. She did little more, however, for subsequently he has fared rather poorly in her literary annals. Only occasionally have Spanish novelists dealt with negro characters. Although *Sab* (1839), by the Cuban Gertrudis Gomez de Avellaneda, has been called "a Spanish *Uncle Tom's Cabin*," the book belongs rather to the New World than to Spain. Yet Spain's service is not to be overlooked; once introduced in her epics and balladry, the negro found a welcome in other parts of Europe.

In France he arrived rather late; and there, as in Spain, he was called a Moor and for long lingered in obscurity and neglect. Not until the closing decades of the eighteenth century did he make any considerable stir—not, in fact, until the humanitarian interest preceding the French Revolution led to a discussion of slavery. Condorcet, Barnave, most of all Montesquieu, joined—sometimes led—the British reformers in damning the slave trade and slavery. During the following century, especially during the eighties and nineties, France was copiously supplied with fiction on provincial American life, and for the first time saw the negro well presented. Moreover, having acquired African colonies, the French came by much knowledge of the natives—knowledge avidly seized upon by novelists and

---

[3] See, for example, Lope de Vega: *El Premio de Bien Hablar* and Cervantes: *El Gallardo Español.*

short story writers. The motif of a visiting African prince, a crude black barbarian bewildered amid the sights of Paris, speedily became popular. Purely literary treatments of the negro had really begun much earlier, however. Napoleon's experiences with the noted Haitian revolutionist, Toussaint L'Ouverture, fascinated many Frenchmen, who wrote long and glorified accounts of the man and his work. It was of this historical episode, for example, that the youthful Victor Hugo wrote in his second romance, *Bug-Jargal* (1826), the hero of which is, naturally enough, a negro. Others who have treated the negro in fiction are Pierre Loti, Madame Blanc Bentzon, and Guy de Maupassant. Present day France is keenly interested in what he is and how he lives—an interest doubtless stimulated by the recent apparance on the battlefields of Europe of negro troops from the French colonies and the United States. The Goncourt Prize for 1922 was awarded René Maran for his *Batouala,* a novel of African savagery which, though severely criticised, proved highly popular.[4]

Naturally French literature produced in the New World has many times told of the slave and the life he lived, especially in Louisiana, where able French-American authors have flourished for more than a century. Dr. C. Testut's *Le Vieux Salomon,*[5] a novel of plantation life before the Civil War, had a wide vogue, despite an unfairness in tone rivalling the account of Simon Legree. A kindlier picture of masters and men appeared in the more ably written *L'Habitation St. Ybars* (1881) of Dr. Alfred Mercier. These are the best known but by no means the only Louisiana novels of their kind.

Germany's experience with the negro largely parallels that of France. The eighteenth century humanitarian concern over slavery was less strongly manifest in Germany than in either France or England; but in the early decades of the following century this sentiment grew rapidly. As the century progressed, fiction dealing with slave conditions was welcomed; still later, after Germany acquired African colonies, her writers turned to the negro in his own land as an interest. German novelists have sometimes laid their scenes in Africa, and naturally have been largely concerned with the natives. But even among German writers, the most significant

---

[4] See also Paul Reboux: *Romulus Coucou,* Paris, 1920.
[5] The book was written in 1858, but not published till 1872.

treatment of the negro has come from men, native sons of the Fatherland, living in the New World and writing for those at home. The founder of this school of German-American romancers was the Austrian, Charles Sealsfield, whose *Lebensbilder aus der westlichen Hemisphaere* (1846) furnished vivid accounts of American social life and provincial types.[6] In his desire to be true to fact Sealsfield went so far as to suggest, by broken, ungrammatical German, the crude vernacular of the slave. Following Sealsfield came Theodor Mügge, who in his *Toussaint* told of the great rebel hero and his struggles to set up a republic on the island of Santo Domingo. Balduin Möllhausen, a worthy successor of Sealsfield, found Southern life his most attractive theme. *Alice Ludlow*[7] has the atmosphere of the Civil War: there is the life on the plantation in which slaves figure conspicuously and the now trite story of the Northern and Southern lovers. In his voluminous writings the negro appears time and time again.[8] Berthold Auerbach[9] and Theodor Storm, however, were native German writers. Auerbach's *Das Landhaus am Rhein* (1869) is the story of a German who threw in his lot with the Americans, first as slave trader, and later as Confederate soldier. Storm's *Von Jenseit des Meeres* (1857) vividly presents the soul-struggle of a mulatto girl—a struggle in which a strong sense of filial duty succumbs to the love of ease and refinement. It is a European treatment of a theme typically American.

England, more than the Continental nations, has been allied to America in thought and spirit and by ties of kinship. Thus it happens that she has been more interested than these others in our provincial types. Furthermore, in her numerous colonies, in Africa and elsewhere, she has met the negro as a problem of her own, and, whether or no, has been compelled to give him attention. Today, especially, her novelists are portraying him as a curious British subject in far away regions of the Empire.

It is, however, a long cry from this present day treatment of

6 See A. B. Faust: *Charles Sealsfield* [a dissertation], Johns Hopkins University, 1892.
7 In *Nord und Süd*, Jena, 1867.
8 See also his *Das Hundertguldenblatt* (1870), *Die Kinder des Sträflings* (1876), *Der Piratenlieutenant* (1870), *Wildes Blut* (1885), *Die Familie Melville* (1889), and *Welche von Beiden?* (1897).
9 For the influence of *Uncle Tom's Cabin* on Auerbach, see MacLean's " Uncle Tom's Cabin " in Germany, 62 ff.

the negro to his debut in England as a Moor. Shakespeare's age confused the negro and Moor[10], and so did the later seventeenth century, by which time the Moor had become a stock type in English literature. In Mrs. Behn's *Oroonoko* (1688), for example, the hero is said to be a Moor, although his complexion is declared to be a " perfect ebony, or polished jet." The story is fictitious— that of an African king kidnapped and sold into West Indian slavery; and while no attempt is made to prove the evils of slavery as an institution, the monstrous injustice meted out to this particular royal captive is insisted upon with the zeal of a reformer. The novel proved so popular that it was dramatized in 1696 by Thomas Southerne and in 1698 by William Walsh. Defoe's *Colonel Jack* (1722)[11] contained a devoted slave; *The Padlock,* a comic opera presented at Drury Lane in 1768, succeeded largely because of the comic servant Mungo; interesting, too, is the fact that when *Robinson Crusoe* was dramatized, in 1781, Friday was represented as an African. As already stated, *Oroonoko* was fiction, but the true narratives of slaves made their appearance in time. Perhaps the most outstanding of these was published in 1734—the narrative of Job, son of an African high priest in Bunda. This man was not only rescued from bondage, but welcomed to England, where an account of his life was written, published in several editions, and read with sympathy from Cornwall to Aberdeen. Again, this was no antislavery document, but these came thick and plentiful with the nineteenth century, when, among others, Wordsworth, Moore, and Elizabeth Barrett Browning joined in the cause. The British antislavery movement was, in fact, hardly less vigorous than our own, culminating in 1834 with the abolition of slavery from the Empire; whereupon the English reformers promptly united with their American brothers in making war on the South's " peculiar institution." In her own struggle. England produced no *Uncle Tom's Cabin;* the belated *Charles Vernon* (1848) of Henry Senior, however, came very near falling into the class. Another novel, Harriet Martineau's *The Hour and the Man* (1840), might be classed as propaganda (written, no doubt, partly for Americans); here the mental and spiritual capacity of the African is glorified—

---

[10] Shakespeare himself called Othello a Moor and described him as negroid.
[11] See also Defoe's *Captain Singleton* (1720), scenes of which are laid in Africa.

a capacity exemplified, so the writer would have it, in the person of Toussaint L'Ouverture. But before the antislavery struggle proper, from about 1800 on, the negro began to serve a more strictly literary use. British romancers discovered in him, and in the Indian, a being unspoiled by civilization, living in that state of nature so much praised by poets of the Wordsworthian school; and novelists—for example, Thackeray—found him a convenient minor character, as have many English authors of recent times: Conrad, Galsworthy, Johnston, and others. To return a moment to the present day, no recent play in English has attracted more notice than Drinkwater's *Abraham Lincoln*—with its "Mr. Custis." Although the dramatist knew too little of Custis's race to portray him vividly, he nevertheless felt the necessity of making the attempt.

But after all is said, no nation except our own has made a masterful presentation of the negro in literature. Only our ablest Southern writers have represented him in lifelike guise, have understood his peculiarities and temper. Europeans, South Americans, writers from the West Indies have discussed him, described him, praised or defended him, yet none of them has shown such intimate knowledge of his life as did Irwin Russell or Joel Chandler Harris.

The American negro is, indeed, not quite the same as his brother in other parts of the world. He is the product of a particular environment, of a peculiar training, of a long and intimate contact with a most vigorous white civilization. He represents today a compromise between his innate savage traits and those new influences which have been cast around him and is thus very different from the chanting savage of the Congo jungles, or for that matter, from the tawny Moor of the European drama, or the sentimental hero of British antislavery verse—most of all, from the misty Ethiopian of the ancients.

To the ancients the negro was impressive because of the romantic haziness with which he was conceived and because he lived in a distant unknown land. Europeans have always regarded him with a kind of interest arising from his color and his evident differences from the white man: not until comparatively recent years have they written of him even sensibly. But Americans, through the sad and unfortunate institution of slavery, have perforce associated with him as have no other whites. From this association they have themselves received much—something, no doubt, from his carefree, irresponsible temper, his irrepressible good humor and musical talent, his unconscious philosophy that the present moment is the all important moment; something, too, from the social and political agitation his mere presence has raised. Gradually he has affected American civilization; gradually, too, he has himself changed from an uncouth savage to the more sophisticated and genial individual of today; and gradually he has won favor as a literary subject. At first unfit for a fictional character, he has at the same time become worthy of favor from the hands of literary men and better understood by them. In the last forty years no character in American fiction has surpassed him in popularity. With the Indian and the frontiersman he shares the honor of being the most original and distinctive contributions which America has yet made to the world's small company of great literary types.

CHAPTER II

THE NEGRO IN COLONIAL LITERATURE

For more than a hundred and fifty years after their settlement in America, the English colonists wrote little that even by courtesy might be termed literature. Raising sufficient food and beating off savage Indians consumed their best energies; moreover, could they have found time, there were few among them able to wield pen for the pleasure of others. Such colonial writings as did come to be published, or have in one way or another been preserved to us, possess for the antiquarian an almost inestimable value, but as literature proper they are of little worth. Accounts of the new world, its wonders, its customs, its people; histories of the various colonies; occasional narratives of adventure among the savages—these and others were the crude output of a frontier civilization. Their chief literary merit—an occasional touch of vigor and quaintness—is insufficient to outweigh their crudity, puerility, and lack of distinction in thought or style. The first serious attempt at literary art was verse, which was small in quantity and tamely imitative of European models; almost the only true poet of the period was Freneau, and he, along with Edwards, Franklin, and the few other notable prose writers, belongs to the closing decades.

For the purposes of this study, the significant fact is that until shortly before the Revolution there flourished no literary form suitable for the realistic presentation of life and manners. Epics, plays, and works of fiction were beyond the poor powers of the colonial writer; moreover, the great literary masterpieces of Europe were conscientiously neglected. No copy of Shakespeare, for example, is known to have found its way to seventeenth century New England; and upon fiction (when it came) the Puritans frowned fiercely, pronouncing it the handiwork of Satan. The clergy, dictators of the public taste, concerned themselves with men principally as beings with souls to save; they had little interest, at least literary interest, in mundane, secular life, in manners, dialects, peculiar or entertaining people, the reaction of character to environment. Nor were conditions much better outside of New England. The other colonists did, it is true, show less austerity of attitude and more avowed interest in worldly sights and concerns, yet they were largely illiterate and had few cities, necessary as

centers of culture if literature was to thrive. The drama and fiction
were nowhere encouraged, and until these could flourish, the negro—
or for that matter, the Indian or the white settler—had small chance
for immortalization as a literary type.

Not that mention of the negro is lacking in colonial writings;
far from it. After the middle of the seventeenth century, European
readers of the crude American publications could hardly fail to
know that slaves were plentiful everywhere—that they were already becoming a disturbing social factor in the New World. References to slavery begin, in fact, with the so-called father of American literature, Captain John Smith, who recorded in his *Generall
Historie of Virginia* (1624): "About the last of August (1619)
came in a dutch man of warre that sold us twenty Negars." Winthrop's *Journal* contains several references. Under date of Febru-
ary 26, 1638, is the entry: " Mr. Pierce, in the Salem ship, the
Desire, returned from the West Indies . . . and brought some cotton, and tobacco, and negroes, etc." In 1645, so Winthrop records,
" One of our ships. . . returned now, and brought wine, and sugar,
and salt, and some tobacco, which she had at Barbadoes, in exchange
for Africoes, which she carried from the Isle of Maio." In the
same year, "The said Mr. James Smith with his mate Keyser were
bound for Guinea to trade for negroes." John Josselyn's *New
England's Rarities Discovered* (1672) contains, among other information, this: that the colonists " are well accommodated with servants . . . of these some are English, others Negroes." Edward Ran-
dolph, writing to the Board of Trade in 1699, conveys the information that in making pitch, tar, turpentine, and raising rice, the
South Carolinians have " about 5,000 Slaves to be employed." He
further relates that "In the year 1686, one hundred Spaniards,
wth. Negroes and Indians, landed at Editoe . . . and broak open the
house of Mr. Joseph Moreton, . . . and carried away . . . all his
money and plate, and 13 slaves, to the value of £1500 sterling. . . .
Two of the Slaves made their escape from thence, and returned
to their master." Mrs. Sarah Kemble Knight, incomparable diarist
and recorder of her trip from Boston to New York in 1704, tells an
anecdote beginning: "A negro slave belonging to a man in the town,
stole a hog's head from his master, and gave or sold it to an Indian,
native of the place." Robert Beverly's *History and Present State
of Virginia* (1705) contains a section on the servants and slaves

in the colony. And the Reverend Mr. Turell, writing a biography of his deceased wife in 1741, praises her for nothing more than that " To her servants she was good and kind, and took care of them, especially of the soul of a slave who died (in the house) about a month before her." These references, typical of the time, are only a few of many; as the century wore on, mention of the negro became even more common. A fair number of references, for example, appear in the balladry of the sixties and seventies. In a Tory ballad deriding Washington and the Americans this stanza occurs:

> The rebel clowns, oh! what a sight!
> Too awkward was their figure.
> 'Twas yonder stood a pious wight,
> And here and there a nigger.[1]

In a preceding stanza is the statement that " The women ran, the darkeys too." In another ballad, this one by the Americans, the British are said to have showered on the colonies, among other blessings, a plentiful supply of savages and rogues, Benedict Arnold chief of all:

> Then in this class of Britain's heroes,
> The Tories, savage Indians, negroes,
> Recorded, Arnold's name shall stand, etc.[2]

Still another contains a humorous account of the capture of General Prescott by the Yankees:

> A tawny son of Afric's race
> Them through the ravine led,
> And entering then the Overing House,
> They found him in his bed.

> But to get in they had no means
> Except poor Cuffee's head,
> Who beat the door down, then rushed in,
> And seized him in his bed.

> " Stop! let me put my breeches on,"
> The general then did pray.
> '' Your breeches, massa, I will take;
> For dress we cannot stay."[3]

---

[1] See Frank Moore: *Ballads of the Revolution*, 100 ff.
[2] Ibid., 334.
[3] [Barney's] *Songs of the Revolution*, 42-43.

Crude, superficial, this treatment is, but it suggests that Cuffee was coming into notice along with another provincial American type, the rustic of " Yankee Doodle." About 1770, too, Colonel Robert Munford's *Candidates* introduced " in Ralpho probably the first negro character in American drama."[4] Finally, it may be pointed out that shortly before this, the precocious versifier, Phillis Wheatley, attracted considerable attention to her race, although not enough to save her from starvation just after the Revolution.

Far more important than these incidental considerations of the negro were the discussions of men opposed to slavery. Throughout most of the eighteenth century there flourished in the colonies a most peculiar antislavery feeling—peculiar in growing, not primarily out of sympathy for the slave, but out of a fear that slavery would indirectly harm the owner class, would lead to sloth, violence of temper, softness; peculiar, too, because held by so many Southerners, who as yet knew nothing of what the cotton gin could effect. The sentiment was not unanimous, of course, else the importation of slaves would have ceased; still many leading colonials were one in desiring all black men back in their own country. While the disgruntled settlers of Georgia were complaining that Oglethorpe had secured the exclusion of slaves from the colony, other settlers, from South Carolina to Massachusetts, were heartily wishing that a like exclusion had been made from the beginning in every settlement. All this interest and discussion was in time to invest the negro with undeniable importance, and lead (as presently to be seen) to considerable literary treatment. A somewhat premature beginning of antislavery activity was made in 1700, when Judge Samuel Sewall published his tract, *The Selling of Joseph*. A curious document, this, in which the old judge shows little understanding of the negro, viewing him through eyes too Puritanical. To him the negro is everything the thrifty New Englander was not, and hence must be a very low order of being—indolent, immoral, dissatisfied, an " unwilling servant." " It may be a question," writes Sewall, "whether all the profits received by negro slaves will balance the account of cash laid out upon them." This argument apparently had little effect, but others put forward by later men met with more favorable reception. By the middle of the eighteenth century, John Hepburn, William Burling, Elihu Coleman, Ralph Sandiford,

---

[4] A. H. Quinn: *A History of the American Drama*, i, 55.

Benjamin Lay, John Woolman, and others, mostly Quakers, had come to oppose slavery on humanitarian grounds alone. Colonel William Byrd, Jonathan Edwards the Younger, Jonathan Boucher, and Henry Laurens likewise denounced the institution in strongest terms. Political leaders began to see in slavery a menace to New World prosperity and well being—an influence weakening to the white race. This was Washington's view, and Jefferson's, both of whom felt, moreover, the inconsistency of holding slaves in a country of boasted freedom and opportunity; Franklin went even further, and founded the first Abolitionist society in America.

All this is evidence of the growing importance of the negro as a problem in the colonies. It is not surprising that as the years passed he should be written of more sympathetically and that finally he should come to the attention of able writers. Before the beginning of our national era, there were various hints of his prominent place in Southern life and some incidental suggestions of the role he was later to take in fiction. No better illustrations could be found, perhaps, than passages in Crèvecœur's *Letters from an American Farmer* (1782), and certain letters of a young South Carolina widow of the Revolutionary War period, Mrs. Eliza Wilkinson.

In the former book, which was in reality a series of essays on American life, the author tells of a visit to a plantation in the neighborhood of Charleston, or "Charles-Town," South Carolina, and of the gay life led by the planters there and of their cruelty to slaves. Although Crèvecœur had much to say on the subject, he understood the negro scarcely at all. Realizing how he himself would feel in the toils of bondage, he invested the slaves with his own thoughts and emotional reactions. His scanty treatment of their qualities, therefore, is little to be praised, although we cannot help commending the righteous indignation he manifested upon the sight of human suffering. The stealing of men from Africa appeared to him an act of monstrous wickedness, and, in spite of the claims of the planters, the owning of them a wrong not sanctioned in the Bible. It was frightful to think of the crimes, the plundering and devastation committed " in some harmless, peaceable African neighborhood, where dwelt innocent people, who even knew not but that all men were black." Later on in the account is the record of a scene the author professed to have witnessed on one of the plantations—a scene in which an unruly slave was literally being eaten alive by birds of prey as he stood tied upright in a cage in the woods. As Crèvecœur tells the story, he handed some water to the suffering wretch, whose eyes the birds had already plucked out. " Tanke you, white man, tanke you," he replied, " pute some poyson and givè me." And then, when asked how long he had been in such a condition: " Two days, and me no die; the birds, the birds, aaah me!" From one point of view Crèvecœur's whole account here is an antislavery argument; ostensibly, however, it was an account of Southern life and peoples. To this shrewd traveller and observer the one outstanding subject in the South, the one sight he remembered vividly and unforgettably, was a vast horde of black men, all classed as chattels, and all with souls and minds and personalities. His crude effort to render the negro dialect is also significant, being among the first attempts of the kind in our literature.

Mrs. Wilkinson likewise scattered bits of dialect through her letters, and although her efforts were no more successful than the feeble one by Crèvecœur, she nevertheless surpassed him in suggesting, for the most part quite unconsciously, the place of the negro in contemporary Southern life. Her main concern in these letters[5] was in describing the hardships inflicted by the British during the invasion of lower South Carolina; but incidentally she sketched a rather complete background of Southern people and manners. Being one of those naive persons of buoyant spirits, with a lively interest in everything, she commented haphazardly on whatever met her eye. There were many types of people around her—brave and courteous Americans, dastardly renegades, positively wicked British invaders, courtly old generals and planters, gay and delicate ladies, and an abundance of negroes everywhere. Through all this assemblage she pursued her animated way, extolling some as friends and heroes, hurling ladylike imprecations at others, seeking refuge in this group or escape from that. But in nothing was she more characteristically Southern than in her attitude toward the slaves. These she felt to be as natural to her world as the air she breathed or the food she ate; it probably never occurred to her effervescent mind that negroes were not especially created to make life easier for her, or indeed that black men had not always been slaves. She was

---

[5] See *Letters of Mrs. Eliza Wilkinson.* . . . Arranged from the Original Manuscripts by Caroline Gilman. New York, 1839.

thoroughly accustomed to them; she could scarcely write a page without introducing them in some way. "A train of Negroes followed with our baggage," she commented, as if this was one of the little incidentals of her life, as indeed it was. Her father, escaping from the British, took " two of his trusty Negro men with him;" no doubt it would have been the same to her if he had taken forty or a hundred, for indeed what were the creatures for if not to follow gladly wherever a patriarchal old planter should lead? Some of them were wholly rascals, she implied; others were very faithful—so faithful that it was a duty to be grateful to them. Sable menials, of one sex or the other, were always in attendance upon her—as protectors, in her flight from the enemy, or as messengers, who like those in the old tragedies enter regularly as bearers of news. At times they were spoken of as intelligent, at other times as dangerous. Most important of all, they were shown to be numerous, to have become a recognized part of New World society.

In no sense, however, were Mrs. Wilkinson's sketches and the other writings in which the negro was mentioned an adequate presentation of him. As a literary subject his possibilities were not seen in colonial times. Even had it been an age of fiction, the negro would probably not have been portrayed immediately upon his arrival in the colonies, for he was somewhat too uncouth for any but gruesomely realistic fiction. He was less attractive at that time than later. He had to develop, to come to his present state through a long abode in a new land. To the colonists, a repulsive and troublesome black man, of lower intelligence than the European, evidently the descendant of the Biblical Ham, and perhaps (it was a debated question then, as later) condemned to slavery by God himself, he was spoken of as a slave, sometimes pitied, but usually considered more a problem to be dealt with than a type of humanity interesting to study. But even then he was leading the life destined to change him into what he became; he was serving an apprenticeship, so to speak, which was in time to gain him full rank in the company of literary characters. Later generations were to understand him and finally place him among the world's noteworthy fictional types. The first years of the Republic were to see the beginnings of this understanding.

CHAPTER III

THE NEGRO CHARACTER IN SERIOUS LITERATURE BEFORE THE CIVIL WAR

I

After the Revolution, in particular after the adoption of the Constitution and the establishment of the Government on a sound financial and political basis, prosperity came to the country surely and swiftly. Wealth increased, and to many it became possible to devote time to literature, music, and the other arts which Europeans had found so conspicuously neglected in our crude settlements. One natural result was a demand for more music and literature, and better. Largely in response to this demand there sprang up a vigorous, if somewhat crude, native drama, which appeared in the larger cities even before the war, and which the hard days of conflict were unable wholly to suppress. This drama was on native American themes, and treated our Indian, our politicians, our land policy, our struggle for freedom. Fiction also came presently to be welcomed, and not only flourished, but advanced apace into the very heart of New England.

With its appearance, the negro crept out from the obscurity of polemical pamphlets, letters, and historical documents into the clear light of day. At first merely mentioned as being on the scene, he next assumed a role as minor character; then shortly he grew to be an interest in and of himself. Within three or four decades after hostilities ceased, his potential literary possibilities, at least such as made for buffoonery and humor, were clearly seen. These possibilities were not adequately utilized, were indeed not fully appreciated, but the fact remains that they were seen: practically all the traits subsequently attributed to him we find foreshadowed in the work of our early novelists. His irrepressible spirits, his complete absorption in the present moment, his whimsicality, his irresponsibility, his intense superstitiousness, his freedom from resentment—all this was suggested, although, be it repeated, not fully or adequately treated. As a mere comic character he was discovered. Unfortunately the same cannot be said for his discovery as a serious type, as a well rounded human being. His subtler characteristics, his deeper emotions, his earnest opinions and aspirations, even his peculiar pathos (so attractive to a later age) were for the most part sadly neglected. True, antislavery versifiers and romancers treated him seriously—in fact, too seriously; but from another cause. In their zeal to show him morally worthy, highly intelligent, possessed of fine emotions, fully equal to and like the white man, they were led into the most egregious blundering of all, and went so wide of the truth as to be ridiculous.

Curiously enough, the reformer who wrote of the negro in order to secure his freedom and the literary artist who found in him a convenient or attractive human type kept each his own way, little regarding the other's presentation. From about 1800 onward to the Civil War their two different and in some ways conflicting treatments flourished side by side, the one thoroughly earnest, impassioned, partisan, the other calm, conventional in manner, incidental to the main purpose of the book; and this with the two seldom so much as bowing as they rubbed elbows. Occasionally a reformer's work proved to have literary merit; such was *Uncle Tom's Cabin,* and such too were some of Whittier's ballads. Occasionally, also, out of the Abolitionist discussion some artist drew inspiration for his work—as did Boucicault for *The Octoroon.* But these were unusual, and as exceptions can be disregarded. Novelists like Simms and Cooke, disdaining to stoop to propaganda, calmly and consistently ignored the problem of slavery in their art proper. Simms stepped aside long enough to pen a heated defense of slavery, but this he set forth for what it was, clearly labelled as a polemical document; upon returning to novel-writing he in no wise changed his picture of slaves or the role assigned them in the story. On the other hand, Abolitionists were too much engrossed in their humanitarian enterprise to regard the dignified requirements of art; if eventually they borrowed the methods of the novelist and dramatist it was only to serve partisan ends, not because they shared the tastes of Poe and Simms and Boucicault.

In order to simplify this study, it seems best to discuss the two treatments separately. The present chapter will be concerned with what serious artists made of the negro character in our literature before the Civil War. The three chapters which follow will contain accounts of how he fared at the hands of Abolitionists and of those who defended slavery.

II

In the literary presentation the British were, as has already been seen, some decades ahead of us. Mrs. Behn's *Oroonoko,* the plays of Walsh and Southerne, Defoe's *Colonel Jack,* Bluet's account of Job, *The Padlock,* all with African characters, precede works of a like kind in America. Furthermore, by 1800, when the negro was still mentioned only incidentally in this country, Englishmen were discovering in him a new literary value, which gained for him considerable notice from romancers of the day. He was made to fill one of the nice demands of a sentimental age—was called upon (with the Indian) to exemplify primitive man, the unspoiled child of nature. Of just such a stamp, for instance, is William Godwin's slave in *St. Leon* (1799). In this novel, a prisoner plans to escape by bribing the negro servant employed around the place. But the servant in question is too faithful to be so corrupted, so that instead of accepting the bribe, he betrays the prisoner to his master, the jailer, who, a product of degenerate civilization, is not so honest, and agrees to take the proffered money himself. Against such baseness the noble black remonstrates:

"Dear master," interposed the negro, "you surely will not listen to the gentleman's offer. When I refused to betray my trust, it is impossible you should consent to betray yours!"
"Hold your tongue, blockhead!" said the other.

And so the disgraceful bargain is made, and the honest servant accused of being exceedingly simple and unfit even for a jail. The reading public of the day evidently enjoyed such scenes, of which there are many.

Although certain American authors were influenced by this conventional British presentation, most of them adopted the negro for a different reason and, without being accurate or thoroughgoing themselves, drew him in more lifelike guise. They at first considered him of no intrinsic importance, but still as too conspicuous a part of the life described in their stories to be omitted. Poe used Jupiter because he had known many a real Jupiter during his boyhood days in Virginia. As far as the requirements of the story go, the servant could have been of any race or color, but Jupiter was a part of Southern life itself, and his presence lent reality to the narrative. Likewise, Simms found slave types frequently useful, and employed them time and again to advance a plot, to help suggest a realistic background, or to set off the praise-worthy qualities of white masters.

Our native fiction once established, and a wide public awaiting treatment of American life, the recognition of the negro as a liter-ary type was almost inevitable. The pioneer novelist, Charles Brockden Brown, occasionally refers to " servants " and " slaves."[1] In Hugh H. Brackenridge's *Modern Chivalry* (1792-1806) a Quaker discusses slavery at some length, and the satirical captain " makes a few remarks on the subject " of purchasing a negro. Irving's fifteenth number of the *Salmagundi Papers* (October 1, 1807) records that in rural America " there is scarce a little hamlet but has one of these old weather-beaten wiseacres of negroes, who ranks among the great characters of the place. . . . Such a sage curmudgeon is old Caesar, who acts as friend Cockloft's prime min-ister or grand vizier; assumes, when abroad, his master's style and title—to wit, Squire Cockloft; and is, in effect, absolute lord and ruler of the soil." Next we are told that besides being "bosom friend and chosen playmate" of the Squire, Caesar is also past master at the art of story-telling, is passionately fond of all the horses, whose pedigrees he knows by heart, is voluminous in con-versation, and in short is as honest and simple an old creature as one will meet on a summer's day.

No better characterization than this appeared till 1821, when Cooper introduced in *The Spy* his own Caesar, a worthy forerunner of many another Caesar, Jupiter, Cato, Hector, soon to follow. From this date on their number rose rapidly. George Tucker's *Valley of Shenandoah* (1824), for example, abounds in slaves, and contains, moreover, a calm, dispassionate discussion of slavery, from the point of view of the Southern planter himself. " We of the present generation," says a planter, "find domestic slavery estab-lished among us, and the evil, for I freely admit it to be an evil, both moral and civil, admits of no remedy that is not worse than the disease." The slave characters themselves, however, are ill-drawn creatures indeed, unconvincing, shadowy. In no way better are those in James E. Heath's *Edge-Hill* (1828) or in Beverly Tucker's *Partisan Leader* (1836). Isabel Drysdale's *Scenes from Georgia* (1827) is more significant, for the Aunt Chloe of this book may be accounted the first successful negro mammy in our fiction.

---

[1] See, for example, *Arthur Mervyn,* i, 141, 158.

Other books of the same class, similarly treating backwoods life in
the South—Longstreet's *Georgia Scenes* (1835), Thompson's *Major
Jones's Courtship* (1840) and *Major Jones's Sketches of Travel*
(1848), Hooper's *Adventures of Captain Suggs* (1845), and Bald-
win's *Flush Times in Alabama* (1853)—also contain passing reference to the negro, although little more.   The best of the group—
Longstreet's *Georgia Scenes*—allows the slave a conspicuous place
in but one brief scene, in which Rose the nurse is vociferously taken
to task by her irate and ill-mannered mistress.

A real landmark in this study, however, and except for *Uncle
Tom's Cabin* the most important single treatment of the negro be-
fore the Civil War, is Kennedy's *Swallow Barn* (1832), a genial,
Addison-like account of life in the Old Dominion.   Kennedy's
literary manner became a model for other Southern novelists—for
Simms, Cooke, Mrs. Gilman, who, along with Poe and Cooper, will
be given more detailed consideration presently.   In the same year
with *Swallow Barn* appeared the *Westward Ho!* (1832) of James
Kirke Paulding, who, himself no Southerner, could yet treat in
Pompey the soon-to-be trite situation of offering a slave his freedom
only to have it cordially refused by the happy man.   In 1834, W. A.
Carruthers published his *Cavaliers of Virginia*, describing the pleas-
ure-loving world of the Virginia gentry, with their elaborate balls,
their sumptuous dinners, their merry hunting of the fox, their kind
treatment of slaves; his later novel, *Knights of the Horseshoe*
(1845), contains, among other characters, old Essex, an early but
ably sketched specimen of the butler type, dignified, respectful yet
critical, with a poise at times disconcerting to those not of the true
plantation aristocracy.   Many and varied are the servants, field
hands, exalted coachmen, domineering mammies who flock through
the pages of Mrs. Gilman's *Recollections of a Southern Matron*
(1837), another landmark in this study and of which more remains
to be said later.   By 1835 Simms was busily engaged on his Southern romances, not surpassed until Cooke joined him two decades
later.   Both men continued their work well beyond the period of the
Civil War.   In 1840 Ingraham's *Quadroone* afforded one of the
earliest graphic treatments of the beautiful slave girl, accursed with
a few drops of African blood.   In the same year Poe published, in
his *Journal of Julius Rodman,* an account of the comical servant
Toby, and three years later, in *The Gold-Bug,* a more interesting.

if still somewhat faulty, one of the faithful bodyguard Jupiter.
The appearance, in 1845, of Zeke in Mrs. Ritchie's play *Fashion*
bore testimony to the influence of the minstrel show upon our literature. On the whole, however, the negro made little headway on
the legitimate stage, remaining consistently in the background, when
he appeared at all, until the dramatization of *Uncle Tom's Cabin*.
In this, and Boucicault's *Octoroon* (1859), he received his most effective dramatic treatment.

As the mid-century approached, the number of presentations of
negro characters grew to be legion. By this time antislavery workers were busily "editing" the autobiographies of runaway slaves,
and composing in verse supposed soliloquies of distressed toilers in
the cotton fields or noble black philosophers in their humble cabins;
a little later they turned to the still more efficacious medium of the
novel, and with Mrs. Stowe as leader flooded the land with accounts
of Southern life and people, both whites and blacks. From still
another source came a second deluge of accounts: from the sentimental romancers, many of them women, who, accepting the tradition of a glamorous feudal South, and a romantic mode of living
there, saw in all this a literary theme highly attractive. Even more
than Kennedy these later authors "threw the glamour of romantic
coloring over all: over the century-old brick mansion with its ornate
approaches, its wings, its doors, its great hall, its spacious rooms,
its antique furniture; over the characters, their dress, conversations,
points of view; over the meals from the bowl of iced toddy an hour
before dinner to the iced wine that followed the dessert; over the
negro quarters, that 'attractive landscape,' the patches of melons
and 'taters; over the whole conduct of life, designed for the attain-
ment of happiness, characterized by thriftless gaiety and by the
flood of hospitality which 'knew no retiring ebb'; over quaint merry-
making and elaborate social functions, over magnificence of manners
and all outward expressions of an inner grace."[2] Such literary material as this was destined to succeed in the age to which it was offered, and succeed it did. All pounced upon it, artist and hack
writer alike, novelist and journalist, John Esten Cooke as well as
T. B. Thorpe, foreigners as well as Americans. The British made
much of it;[3] the Germans of the school of Sealsfield came under

---

2 F. P. Gaines: *The Southern Plantation*, 22.

3 Note, for example, G. P. R. James: *The Old Dominion* (1856); and
M. E. Braddon: *The Octoroon* (1862).

its spell;[4] nor did Mrs. Stowe herself escape. *Uncle Tom's Cabin,* denunciation of slavery as it is, nevertheless sets forth much about Southern society in no unpleasant light.

Typical of the sentimental romancers was Mrs. E. D. E. N. Southworth, who gilded her pictures of *ante-bellum* society with a zeal which reminds one of Page and Gordon, later.[5] Her slaves are hilariously happy—all except the quadroon Henny, of *Retribution* (1849), who suffers cruelly at the hands of her jealous young mistress. Of a like temper was Mrs. Mary J. Holmes, whose *Tempest and Sunshine* (1854) and *Meadow Brook* (1857) are thoroughly conventional in manner, following closely the fashion exemplified in Mrs. Southworth. Other examples are Mrs. Hentz's *Marcus Warland* (1852), *The Planter's Northern Bride* (1854), and the anonymous *Dew Drop of the Sunny South* (1858), all proslavery in tone and typical of a large class of books appearing after the publication of *Uncle Tom's Cabin.* Following the tradition, and yet avoiding its worst superficialities, was Robert Goulding's *Young Marooners* (1852), a boys' story with an old nurse, Judy, portrayed straight from life. Likewise superior is D. H. Strother's *Virginia Illustrated* (1857), "that early and delightful chronicle of Virginia life," as Page called it. General Strother was non-partisan, and excellent as was his whole performance, it excels especially in the portrayal of slave types. Hardless less commendable are Tucker's *Hansford* (1857), the romance of an earlier epoch, Hungerford's *Old Plantation* (1857), a second *Swallow Barn,* abounding in sunny sketches of the black folk, who speak a consistent dialect, and Victor's *Maum Guinea's Children* (1861), which centers interest on life in the slave quarters during the Christmas season.

Not only in these narratives of Southern life, but sometimes in unexpected places, far afield, the negro puts in an appearance. Rose-Water of Melville's *White Jacket* (1850), a sea story far removed from the novel of domestic life, boasts that his mother was the mistress of a planter. Henry A. Wise's sensational *Captain Brand of the "Centipede"* (1860), likewise a sea story, borrows from the plantation tradition such characters as the negress Babette, the ebony pilot, Peter Crabreef, and heroic Banou. Most surprising of all, however, is to find Nathaniel Hawthorne concerned with

---

4 See Chapter I.
5 See especially *Shannondale* (1850) and *Virginia and Margaret* (1852).

negro characters.   In addition to his hint in *The Marble Faun* (1860) that Miriam might be the daughter of a West Indian planter, by an octoroon mistress, there is in *The House of the Seven Gables* (1851) a black servant of the Pyncheon family, Scipio by name, who not only takes part in the narrative, but speaks a kind of half-hearted dialect.   One scrap of dialogue suggests that the usually sedate Hawthorne was tempted by the humorous possibilities in Scipio.   The negro asks Matthew Maule, the carpenter, "And what for do you look so black at me?"   Whereupon the other responds, "No matter, darky.   Do you think nobody is to look black but yourself?"   Scipio, however, is such a vague and misty figure that he deserves mention only because of the greatness of his originator; but that Hawthorne, who usually avoided the superficial aspects of realism, and eschewed provincial types and dialect, would depict him at all eloquently testifies to the hold the negro had by this time secured on the literary world.

During the years from 1840 onward a goodly crop of magazines flourished in this country, and in them, especially in those founded in the fifties, appeared numerous novels, tales, and sketches of society in the slaveholding states.   Conservative editors sternly rejected anything savoring of propaganda, yet this in no wise excluded the fiction so plentifully furnished by the school of Mrs. Southworth—fiction showing the conventional old planter, irritable and aristocratic, the capriciouly bewitching heroine, his daughter, the pert young scion of the family, his son, the faithful Cato, the domineering mammy, the capering pickaninnies.   Such novels and stories filled the pages of *Harper's*, of *Graham's*, and of *Putnam's;* for some time *The Union Magazine* published steadily each month one or more such pieces; while *The Southern Literary Messenger,* the chief literary organ of the South, naturally opened its pages to stories following the plantation tradition, publishing in serial issues complete novels and romances.[6]   All told, so numerous were these

---

6 There follow but a few of the many references possible to make here: they were chosen almost at random.   *Harper's*: Feb., 1851, "The Kafir Trader" (a story of Africa); Sept., 1853, "A Cruise after and among the Cannibals"; and in the latter issue, an installment of Strother's "Virginia Illustrated."   *Graham's*: Nov. and Dec., 1856, "Cecele Vannier," by Mrs. Helen Maria Arion; note the conventionally drawn nurse, old Winnie.   *Putnam's*: Nov., 1855, Dec., 1855, "The Virginia Springs," a story of Virginia life, with negro characters and dialect.   *The Union Magazine*: Oct., 1847, "The Swamp Ghost at Christmas," by Mary S. B. Dana; Jan., 1848, "The Bewildered Savage," by L. Maria Child; Feb., 1848, "It Grows as It

narratives that to do justice to the entire group would be impossible; here it is sufficient to call attention to their number and uniform lack of distinction. They added nothing to the treatment of the negro, but at best merely called attention to a literary type already well established.

During the whole period, and even earlier, negro minstrelsy had come into prominence, introducing to many audiences in America and Europe the Snowball, the Jim Crow, the Dandy Jim of the comic stage. Without being itself in any way literary, the minstrel performance left a clear, and on the whole direful, impression upon our fiction and balladry. Incidentally, it left us our best loved body of songs, mostly by Stephen Collins Foster—melodies taken up by our whole nation, cherished by us with a fondness usually accorded only the folk song, and despite their relatively small negroid ingredient, persistently and almost universally held to be representative of the negro in sentiment and musical genius. More important here, minstrelsy affected the literary concept of the negro; it called undue attention to his humorous traits and attributed to him others never his—never, perhaps, properly belonging to any human being. By overstressing these comical traits, it accentuated a tendency, already too pronounced, to view him superficially, to brand him as a hopeless and soulless buffoon. Upon the whole, therefore, minstrelsy has had a regrettable influence: the negro still suffers, off stage and on, from the frivolous presentations of the black-faced comedians.[7]

If, however, the minstrel concept was superficial, crude, mis-representative, so in a lesser degree were the characterizations of our ablest writers before the Civil War. In one way or another they all fell short—most in considering their subject too exclusively comic or in making him a wooden puppet. Nevertheless, either because the performance was rich in suggestions and promise for the future (as was Mrs. Gilman's) or because of the greatness of the writer himself (as with Poe), the work of several authors merits

Goes," by Mrs. E. F. Ellet; April, 1848, "The Lost Glove," by Jane C. Camp-bell; July, 1848, "Southern Sketches," by Mary S. B. Dana. *The Southern Literary Messenger*: in 1835, the novel "Lionel Granby," which insists upon the happiness of slaves; in 1839, "Judith Bensaddi," in which the Abolition heroine is converted; in 1848, "The Two Country Houses," by Philip Pendle-ton Cooke, containing vivid descriptions of the hospitable life of rural Virginia.

[7] For the best account of negro minstrelsy, see Brander Matthews: "The Rise and Fall of Negro Minstrelsy," *Scribner's Magazine*, June, 1915.

more attention than has been possible, thus far, to give in this brief
sketch. Accordingly there follows a somewhat more detailed discussion of the presentations of Cooper, Kennedy, Mrs. Gilman,
Poe, Simms, and Cooke.

III

The world over, James Fenimore Cooper is remembered as the
creator of Uncas, of Chingachgook, and of other noble Indians;
it is scarcely known, however, that he was the first of our great
authors to portray a distinctive African character—Caesar of *The
Spy* (1821). As a pioneer, in this field as in describing Indians,
Cooper did remarkably well. He treated the African type not
perfectly or exhaustively, but nevertheless with imaginative sympathy. He not only sides with Cora Munro,[8] the unfortunate girl
of partial slave blood, but also with black Caesar, who, though an
indulged menial, is still pitiable in his servile condition. " The faithful old black," he tells us, had " been reared from infancy in the
house of his master," and " as if in mockery of his degraded state,
had been complimented with the name of Caesar." Further, upon
Caesar's being offended by the pedlar, Harvey Birch, the following
dialogue ensues:

"A black man so good as white, Miss Sally," continued the
offended negro, "so long as he behave heself."

"And frequently he is much better," rejoined his mistress.[9]

The author's own opinions are at times expressed outright, as for
instance: " It is one of the curses of slavery, that its victims become
incompetent to the attributes of a freeman." Again, Caesar himself
remarks, "If dere had nebber been a man curious to see Africa,
dere would be no colour people out of deir own country." This particular kind of sympathy, this implied contention that the blacks
were as good as their masters, the Southern authors, humane though
many were, never displayed.

In the character of Cora Munro, Cooper recognized and deliberately treated as an important interest the problem of the luckless white mildly tainted with African blood. Cora is one of
Cooper's few tolerable heroines, brave, self-possessed, the opposite

---

[8] In *The Last of the Mohicans* (1826). Other negro characters are found
in *The Pioneers* (1823) and *The Red Rover* (1828).

[9] *The Spy*, 43.

of her silly, helpless half-sister, yet sensitive and moody. Because of her peculiar actions the reader recognizes immediately that in her life something is amiss. She persists in keeping her veil on, and when some one intimates that because of his darker color the Indian guide is inferior to Europeans, she flares up in quick resentment. In time all this is made clear; we learn that her West Indian mother had had, somewhere back in the past, an African ancestor and had thus bequeathed to her daughter the curse of an inferior race. The problem suggested in Cora Munro, however, Cooper refused to work out thoroughly, choosing to avoid the difficulty by having a savage murder the girl. Whether he would have advocated Cora's actually marrying a white man remains a question.[10]

Caesar Thompson, as Mr. Wharton's old slave insisted upon calling himself, offered no such perplexing problem, but was more difficult to portray. Although serious enough in this characterization, Cooper fell into the early mistake of seeing in Caesar a being unduly comical. To picture him in a humorous light was in itself no sin against art; rather the error lay in going to an extreme, in resorting to caricature, in insisting too strongly on what was doubtless fundamentally true. This description will serve admirably for illustration:

> ...In person, Caesar was short, and we should say square, had not all the angles and curves of his figure bid defiance to anything like mathematical symmetry. His arms were long and muscular, and terminated by two bony hands, that exhibited on one side, a coloring of blackish grey, and on the other, a faded pink. But it was in his legs that nature had indulged her most capricious humour. There was an abundance of material injudiciously used. The calves were neither before nor behind, but rather on the outer side of the limb, inclining forward, and so close to the knee as to render the free use of that joint a matter of doubt. In the foot, considering it as a base on which the body was to rest, Caesar had no cause of complaint, unless, indeed, it might be that the leg was placed so near the centre, as to make it sometimes a matter of dispute, whether he was not walking backwards.[11]

In making Caesar superstitious, timorous, and often ludicrously dignified, Cooper was at least on the right track. Overdrawn

---

[10] The love of the noble Indian, Uncas, for Cora is perhaps Cooper's best treatment of romantic attachment; he made much of it. Cora's death occurs, however, before the affair reaches an advanced stage.

[11] *The Spy,* 36.

though the character seems, since Caesar was supposedly a pampered slave, this concept was nearer actuality than the virtuous, if somewhat swarthy, Sir Galahad of British romancers or the sighing philosopher of antislavery verse. If we make due allowance for the early date of the novel, the literary tastes of the day, and the state of fiction, Caesar appears more natural than we might expect. Faulty in detail, he is in the large true to life—no Uncle Remus, to be sure, but still, more lifelike than many a later fictional negro. A spoiled old man, petulant, superstitious, with an abiding faith in ghosts, unduly pompous, fond of bright colors, he is one of a primitive race which civilization has not entirely altered. He believes in keeping out of the way of bullets; he cannot be convinced that Harvey Birch's father did not arise from the bed in which he had just expired; he admires the white aristocracy and looks down upon the poor whites with unfeigned contempt; he is thoroughly panic-stricken when caught taking the place of his young master, who is escaping from military prison. On the other hand, he is always faithful to the family of which he is proud to consider himself a part, and although easily offended even by Mr. Wharton or his children, he bears no lasting resentment. His whole attitude toward life is primitive. Conventional some of these traits and actions have come to be; nevertheless they are founded on fact.

IV

John Pendleton Kennedy was by far the most pleasing of our early writers on Southern life, and in his leisurely style and good-natured attitude toward the world, reminds one much of his friend, Washington Irving. *Swallow Barn, or Life in the Old Dominion* (1832) shows evident kinship with " Knickerbocker's " *History* and *The Sketch Book*. If in temper, however, he suggests Irving, in theme at least Kennedy reminds one more of Page. There is this difference between the two men, though : Kennedy drew principally on observation, was more leisurely, and idealized his pictures with a less conscious pen; Page, on the other hand, though a better story teller, was writing with a glorified concept of the past, or from memory or hearsay. Kennedy's negroes are forerunners of those of Page; they are types, too often stock types, and at times their function in the story is largely mechanical. Note, for instance, old Carey, in charge of the horses, "who, in his reverence for the occupation, is the perfect shadow of his master." "Carey thinks he knows a great deal more upon the subject than his master, and their frequent intercourse has begot a familiarity in the old negro almost fatal" to the master's supremacy.   How many such Careys were to follow!   But unlike Page, Kennedy uses dialect hardly at all, a difference which counts heavily in the balance.   Yet this difference aside, Page has little advantage over his predecessor. Kennedy probably came much nearer to truth in spirit.

Swallow Barn recounts how the New Yorker, Mark Littleton, yields to the long continued supplications of his Virginia cousins to visit them.   In the introductory epistle (written supposedly to a Northern friend) he acknowledges having fallen in love with the country, and notes with deep interest all the strange and delightful features of Southern life—the lovable and interesting types of people, the hospitality and easy manners of the landholders, their thoughts and ideals, the life they lead, and the agreeable and sometimes amusing sights on the great estates.   Foremost among these sights are the slaves, of whom there are many kinds and descriptions: old Carey, the privileged groom, who lords it over his fellows and at times even over his master; " broad-shouldered, dwarfish " Uncle Jeff, who insists upon giving advice on how to cure sprains; big Ben, in all his glory when directing the nocturnal quest for the " shocking fat " 'possum which had wrought havoc among the poultry; joyous Ganymede, characteristically elated at delivering the invitation to dinner at the big house; the amusing and carefree pickaninnies, each with but one garment, a shirt; and a number of others, all naively primitive in their outlook on the world.

Kennedy has his own manner of putting negro characters before us—not by allowing them to reveal themselves in dialect, but by having some planter or the letter-writer himself give us an estimation.

> " That, sir," said Meriwether, " is no less a person than Jupiter.   He is an old bachelor, and has his cabin here on the hill.   He is now near seventy, and is a King of the Quarter. He has a horse, which he extorted from me last Christmas; and I seldom come here without finding myself involved in some new demand, in consequence of my donation. . ."[12]

This passage typifies many another in the book.

As already noted, very little dialect is employed.   The charac-

---

[12] *Swallow Barn,* 452.

ters who speak more than a few words usually do so in good English. Except for an occasional phrase or a word like " fotch," Kennedy rarely attempts the negro idiom, and even when he does so, is inconsistent, mingling dialectal expressions and the most excellent of English. "God bless you, master Harvey, and young gentlemen all!" exclaims Carey, but he adds, as he retires with many formal bows, "Good night, *gemmen."* Kennedy describes his negroes delightfully and convincingly, but he cannot make them speak, so that however lifelike they appear before, the minute they open their mouths they cease to be natural. Only Uncle Jeff, who incidentally has little to say, talks somewhat as he should, and his dialect is commendable principally in being better than that of the others.

The author must have realized his shortcomings, for more than once he admits reporting in good English what was really spoken in a vernacular peculiar to the negro. One of the slaves, for instance, had just been entertaining the ladies. "And in this strain," remarks the author, " clothed in his own dialect, he rehearsed, in a doggerel ballad." The text continues:

> It will not do to give his words, which, without the aid of all the accessories, the figure of the old man himself, and the rapid twang of his banjo, and especially the little affectations of his professorial vanity, would convey but a bald impression of the serio-comic effect the whole exhibition had upon us.[13]

Such an evasion Kennedy was doubtless wise in preferring to badly imitated negro speech. Finally may be noted a favorite trick of his, of mingling occasional dialectal terms with his own words to give a touch of local color. For instance, we are told that "the boys had *diskivered* him (to use Carey's own term)," and that in discussing the hunt "Carey affirmed with a 'howsomdever' " many things about 'possums.

Worse than this weak employment of dialect was Kennedy's taking the negro race too much for granted, viewing them superficially, seeing in them merely an inferior people, amusing, tractable, fortunate in being associated with a master class holding them in easy bondage. His one narrative in which slaves are the sole heroes, the account of Aunt Lucy and her son Abe, near the end of the book, fails dismally. At best he set forth only the superficial

---

[13] Ibid., 103.

aspect of the race; his commentary can never be called profound, although practically always delightful to read. The following description of a dining room scene will serve for illustration:

> A bevy of domestics, in every stage of training, attended upon the table, presenting a lively type of the progress of civilization, or the march of the intellect; the veteran waitingman being well-contrasted with the rude half-monkey, half-boy, who seemed to have been for the first time admitted to the parlor; whilst, between these two, were exhibited the successive degrees that mark the advance from the young savage to the sedate and sophisticated image of the old-fashioned negro nobility. It was equal to a gallery of caricatures, a sort of scenic satire upon man in his various stages, with his odd imitativeness illustrated in the broadest lines. Each had added some article of coxcombry to his dress; a pewter buckle fastened to the shirt for a breast pin; a dingy parti-colored ribbon, ostentatiously displayed across the breast, with one end lodged in the waistcoat pocket; or a preposterous cravat girding up an exorbitantly starched shirt collar, that rivalled the driven snow, as it traversed cheeks as black as midnight, and fettered the lower cartilage of a pair of refractory, raven-hued ears. One, more conceited than the rest, had platted his wool (after a fashion common amongst the negroes) into five or six short cues both before and behind; whilst the visages of the whole group wore that grave, momentous elongation which is peculiar to the African face, and which is eminently adapted to express the official care and personal importance of the wearer.[14]

Profound or not, these remarks are evidently the work of one thoroughly accustomed to such scenes as are here described, and one, moreover, who delighted in them and wished others also to delight.

Swallow Barn may rightly be considered the most genially written, the most fair tempered, the most artlessly artistic, if withal not perfect, treatment the negro received before the Civil War.

V

Second only to *Swallow Barn* was Mrs. Caroline Gilman's *Recollections of a Southern Matron* (1838), an enthusiastically written account of the experiences of a Northern woman upon settling in Charleston, South Carolina. The book glories in the intense pride of the Southerners, in their love-makings, their duels, their manners and habits, their haughtiness and abandon—all of which

---

[14] *Swallow Barn,* 327.

is set forth with plentiful Victorian sentiment. More than on anything else interest centers on the slaves. Perhaps, for one reason, because they were new to her, Mrs. Gilman rejoiced in them, making copious notes on their dialect and habits, introducing them on almost every page, frequently having them speak. Their dialect she reported well, much better, in fact, than most of her contemporaries among Southern authors. Undoubtedly a close observer, she appears to have copied down their actual words, not trusting wholly to memory to recall what was said. In one note, for instance, is the statement, "This touching prayer was heard by the writer."

The role Mrs. Gilman assigns the negro in Southern society is important. Inferior though he is, a natural servant, he is nevertheless human, a highly useful menial, and, as long as he stays in his place, worthy of the friendship and protection of the whites. One slaveholder goes so far as to risk his life in saving an old negress from the flames of a burning building. The relations between slave and master are shown to be in every way ideal. Not least among the slave's functions is amusing his master; the whites enjoy the unwitting humor in a Cato or Hector, and because of his presence find their world a more pleasant and habitable abode. Of the comical aspect of African character, Mrs. Gilman made much, as can be seen from the following somewhat exaggerated description of a negro wedding:

> ...The ceremony was to be performed by Friday, their religious *leader*. This man had been, many years before, suddenly converted while ploughing, and the evidence seemed satisfactory by the number of followers he obtained. He lived up to his profession for a considerable period, but the hour of temptation came; a theft in the smoke-house was traced to him, and he was immediately deserted by the people, who chose a leader of more consistent practice. Subsequently Friday repented, reformed, and got religion again, as he said, at the plough, at the same spot where the first call had been given. Being reinstated in his office, he was invited to unite the happy couple.
>
> The bride and her attendants appeared with the little finery that we could gather from our country toilets.
>
> Friday, nothing daunted by our presence, commenced a prayer, which was followed by an exhortation to the pair before him on their duty; then, turning to the groom, he said—
>
> "Bacchus, you been guine marry dis woman for lub or for money?"

"For lub, sir," replied Bacchus, bowing, half to the pro-
pounder, and half to the bride.

"Sheba," said Friday to the lady, "you been guine for marry
dis man for lub or for money?"

"For lub, sir," replied Sheba, courtesying modestly.

"Den," said Friday, "I pernounce you man and wife, and
wish you many happy return! Salute de bride!" Upon which
the lips of Bacchus resounded on the lips of Sheba like the
Christmas cannon. We all shook hands with her, and a dance
in the kitchen, under Diggory's direction, concluded their evening's amusement.[15]

This passage represents fairly accurately Mrs. Gilman's level.
If on the one hand she seldom rose above it, on the other she rarely
dropped below, so that, both in style and characterization, the ex-
tract may be said to typify her work.

VI

Other critics besides Mr. Stedman have detected, or believed
they have detected, in the poetry of Edgar Allan Poe traces of negro
influence. In view of this, it is especially significant to find Poe
making use of several negroes in his tales, all the more so because
of his usual avoidance of realism in locality and character.

Poe's earliest negro character was Pompey of *A Predicament*
(1838), a creature utterly fantastic and impossible. In *The Journal of Julius Rodman* (1840), however, a fictitious record of the
first journey by white men over the Rockies, appears one Toby,
"not the least important personage in our party," says the chronicler,
and "as ugly an old gentleman as ever spoke—having all the peculiar features of his race; the swollen lips, large white protruding
eyes, flat nose, long ears, double head, pot-belly, and bow legs."
The old slave gets the party into a humorous difficulty with the far-
Western Indians, who are wonderstricken at his sooty appearance.
Acting somewhat out of character, the red men boldly attack the
explorers in order to get a closer view of Toby.

...They had never before seen or heard of a blackamoor, and
it must therefore be confessed that their astonishment was not
altogether causeless. . . . Upon relating their adventures to their
companions, the two savages [who had discovered Toby] could
obtain no credit for the wonderful story, and were about losing
caste for ever, as liars and double-dealers, when they proposed

---

[15] *Recollections of a Southern Matron*, 125-6.

to conduct the whole band to the boats by way of vindicating their veracity. The sudden attack seemed to have been the mere result of impatience on the part of the still incredulous Assiniboins; for they never afterwards evinced the slightest hostility, and yielded up the piroque as soon as we made them understand that we would let them have a good look at old Toby. The latter personage took the matter as a very good joke, and went ashore at once, *in naturalibus,* that the inquisitive savages might observe the whole extent of the question. Their astonishment and satisfaction were profound and complete. At first they doubted the evidence of their own eyes, spitting upon their fingers and rubbing the skin of the negro to be sure that it was not painted. The wool of the head elicited repeated shouts of applause, and the bandy legs were the subject of unqualified applause. A jig dance on the part of our ugly friend brought matters to a climax. Wonder was now at its height. Approbation could go no farther. Had Toby but possessed a single spark of ambition he might then have made his fortune for ever by ascending the throne of the Assiniboins, and reigning as King Toby the First.[16]

In this passage attention is directed rather to situation than to character, and Toby is intended, first and principally, to make us laugh.

In portraying Jupiter, the faithful servant of Mr. Legrand in *The Gold-Bug* (1843), Poe was more serious, although hardly more successful. A free negro, affectionately dubbed "Jup" by his "Massa Will," whom he refuses to leave, Jupiter is an admirable exemplification of slave virtues, and is of some importance in the story. The character, however, is unconvincing, being far too simple and naive, and full of the most surprising contradictions. He is able to look out for his master, and yet cannot tell his right hand from his left. Although a devoted menial, well knowing his place, he actually prepares a club with which to discipline the wayward Legrand. A practiced realist might have saved the situation by having Jupiter do this as a sort of good-natured prank, but Poe's attempt falls flat and is a contradiction of character. After finishing the story, one feels Jupiter to be, all too glaringly, the careless product of a romancer's pen.

Least of all does his speech ring true. He speaks, not indeed like an educated white, but a confused jumble of good English and

---

[16] Virginia ed. of Poe's works, iv, 84-5.

dialect never heard on earth. Occasional expressions like "dis here pissel" (this here epistle), "dan" (than), "tote" (for carry), "gwine" (am going) are after the true manner of Jupiter's race; moreover, such lines as "De crows done gobble ebery bit of de meat off" and "How I know? why, he talk about it in he sleep—dat's how I nose"—these are passable, but the best that can be found. Nor does Jupiter's being a Charleston negro explain this peculiar vernacular. An examination of the vernacular in question shows that Poe was reporting very crudely the speech of the Virginia slave.

That he reported it at all, however, or yielded to the literary influences of the day and placed a negro character in the story, must in itself count for something. In this one presentation, at least, he was distinctly American and Southern.

VII

If Cooper was the first, and Kennedy the most genial, William Gilmore Simms was the most persistent creator of negro characters among our early literary men. Of these writers he alone made repeated use of fictional slaves, admitting them into practically all his romances, written over a period of some thirty years.[17] Kennedy had employed them to lend verisimilitude to pictures of Southern society; Simms went further, and in addition to this assigned them necessary parts in the action—used them as military guides, sent them into battle, had them protect the women and children left in their care. They are of many kinds, ranging in mold from the inconsequential black who happens to be on the spot to the brave and intelligent freeman. With Simms, in fact, a negro might be anything short of the central heroic figure—a stubbornly devoted ally who refuses to betray a master, a valuable aid to some hard-pressed general, the trusted friend of a dashing young cavalier, but never quite an Othello or a swarthy Tamerlane.

The slave heroic was a favorite with Simms, and of the type he made frequent and constant use. Such were Hector of *The Yemassee,* Tom of *The Partisan,* Scipio of *Mellichampe,* Braugh of *Southward Ho!*—men who save their masters' lives, prove excellent mili-

---

[17] See especially *Guy Rivers* (1834), *The Yemassee* (1835), *The Partisan* (1835), *Mellichampe* (1836), *Border Beagles* (1840), *The Wigwam and the Cabin* (1845-6), *The Forayers* (1855).

tary scouts, or come almost to the point of being hanged before be-
traying a trust. The trouble with these characters is that, in their
heroic mood, they appear utterly artificial—about as convincing as
the idealized knight-errant of medieval romance. They become real
only in their less ambitious moments when, in camp or at home, they
amuse their white friends by making naive comments on the world,
or, better still, when they join in the rejoicing of their humbler
fellow slaves who are never anything but unpretentious menials.

These humbler folk, of whom there are a multitude, serve to
make more convincing the realistic background against which the
story moves; or they furnish uproarious comedy through their
ultra-simplicity or whimsicality. When serving the latter function
they are usually at their best. In *Guy Rivers,* for instance, a master
calls upon an extremely cautious slave for help in establishing an
alibi:

". . .Hob—Hob—Hob—where the devil are you? Hob—
say, you rascal, was I within five miles of the Catcheta Pass
to-day?" The negro—a black of the sootiest complexion—
now advanced—
   " No, mosser."
   " Was I yesterday? "
The negro put his finger to his forehead, and the lawyer
began to fret at this indication of thought, and, as it promised
to continue, exclaimed—
   " Speak, you rascal, speak out—you know well enough,
without reflecting." The slave cautiously responded—
   " If mosser want to be dere—mosser dere—no 'casion for
ax Hob."
   " You black rascal, you know well enough I was not there—
that I was not within five miles of the spot, either to-day, yesterday, or for ten days back."
   " Berry true, mosser—if you no dere, you no dere. Hob
nebber say one ting when mosser say 'noder."
The unfortunate counsellor, desperate with the deference
of his body servant, now absolutely perspired with rage;
while, to the infinite amusement of all, in an endeavor to strike
the pliable witness, who adroitly dodged the blow, the lawyer,
not over-active of frame, plunged incontinently forward, and
paused not in his headlong determination until he measured
himself at length on the ground.[18]

But whether obsequious like Hob here, or brave like Hector,

18 *Guy Rivers,* i, 255-6.

Simms's fictional negroes always appear happy, well treated, on the whole fortunate in bondage.   They desire freedom so little that they refuse it when offered, preferring the humane governance and protection of a white planter, always ready to take their part.   Such a master is Porgy of *The Partisan*, who will allow no man to kick Tom but himself:

> "That's Tom's voice—I'll swear it among a thousand; and somebody's beating him!   I'll not suffer that."   And with the words he moved rather rapidly away toward the spot whence the noise proceeded.
>
> "Don't be in a hurry now, Porgy; remember—keep cool, keep cool, keep cool," cried Humphries, as he followed slowly after the now hurrying philosopher. . . .
>
> "Nobody shall kick Tom while I'm alive.   The fellow's too valuable for blows;—boils the best rice in the southern country, and hasn't his match, with my counsel, at terrapin in all Dorchester.   Holla! there, my friend, let the negro alone, or I'll astonish you."[19]

These last remarks are, of course, spoken in jest, but behind them lurks the unmistakable import of a truth: Tom is dear to his master—the most happy relationship exists between master and man.

Once, at least, Simms made the negro a chief and self-sufficient literary interest—in *The Lazy Crow*,[20] a story said to be based on first hand information.   Scipio, the indulged slave of Mr. Carrington, finds himself, so he complains, bewitched by Gullah Sam, an old African believed by the superstitious plantation populace to be a magician.   Of how poor Scipio almost dies of the illness caused by fright and the terrors of imagination, of how he is saved by another magician, Methuselah, of the mysterious tricks performed by this Methuselah to cast off the evil spell from the victim, of the shooting of the old black crow which has haunted Scipio, of the complete discomfiture of Gullah Sam, of the attitude of the black folk toward the whole mysterious sequence of events, and of many traits of the negroes themselves, the story treats at length.   The main actors are the slaves themselves, whom no white hero thrusts into the background; nor is the story primarily humorous, but rather the serious elaboration of a situation growing out of superstition among people primitive almost to the point of savagery.   Incidentally, the dialect is of a higher order than that usual with

---

[19] *The Partisan*, 424.
[20] In the volume, *The Wigwam and the Cabin*.

Simms. Perhaps the individual characters, like Scipio or Methuselah, are no more penetratingly presented than others, but certainly the author nowhere else approaches this story as a broad consideration of negro psychology and idiosyncrasies.

Considering the intense interest shown in *The Lazy Crow,* and that through many years Simms continued to utilize slave characters, his eye ever on them as he penned romance after romance of the South, we cannot but wonder at the small advance he made. The years seemed to teach him little. If 'Bram and Little Peter of *The Forayers* show some improvement over Hector of *The Yemassee,* the difference can be accounted for alone on the score of years of sheer practice in portraying the type. To the end Simms continued to be superficial and careless. To the end he made some of his black characters mock heroes, puppets of the most wooden kind, drew all of them inconsistently, and put in their mouths dialect utterly impossible, full of the grossest artificialities. Simms never improved greatly on the dialect of his early days, in which occur such absurd jumbles as the following: "I can't help it, missis—I must go. I hab hand and foot—I hab eye for see—I hab toot for bite—I 'trong, missis, and I must go look for Maussa." From a Southerner, accustomed every day to the talk of slaves, we might reasonably expect more than this. But as a matter of fact, defective dialect was only one of the author's several literary shortcomings. He was crude in all his artistic efforts—especially so in portraying characters, both white and black. Writing a kind of unpolished romance, in which fictional people use high-flown diction and undergo numerous sensational experiences, he laid emphasis, not upon the subtle qualities of the human mind or soul, but upon action, situation. Remembering this, we should not expect to find in his books the standard of a Joel Chandler Harris. In the present study, his chief significance lies in the repeated and persistent use he made of the negro character, suggesting as he did the literary importance of the type, and promising better things for it in future.

VIII

It is disappointing, and at first a little puzzling, to find the Virginia novelist, John Esten Cooke, slighting the negro. It would almost seem as though, disdaining to notice the Abolitionist novelists outright, he nevertheless made them indirect answer by this neglect, implying that the slave was by no means the South's chief concern. However that may be, Cooke was not averse to portraying the Indian, a provincial type of which he was fond but about which he knew little at first hand. In *The Last of the Foresters* (1856), the white heroine Redbud loves Verty, a youth believed to have some Indian blood in his veins; and although Verty proves eventually to be a white man, the long lost son of a planter, Redbud had considered marrying him before this fact was known. Such a possibility on her part shocks Cooke not at all, apparently; but how, one is inclined to ask, if Verty had been partly negro? The answer is all too obvious.

Since in ignoring the existence of slaves, he would have sinned against the life portrayed, Cooke incidentally introduced them into his stories. He ushers them on the scene, has them play brief parts, and then pushes them into the background, or removes them, that the white actors may receive undivided attention. " Dozens of negroes," runs one of his descriptions, "ranging from little ebon balls, clad in unmentionable costumes, to the stately white-haired Catos and Dinahs, pass about from out-house to out-house."[21] A young gentleman is taking his ease in his room: " ' My book,' says he to a negro boy, who has just brought in some dishes."[22] Now, and again, the author steps out and makes some comments in his own person, as for instance the following remarks on the plantation mammy:

> In the South, and more especially in Virginia, that element of society denominated "Mammy," is of no slight importance and dignity.

> This lady is of high aristocratic dignity. She is of the Order of the " Bath "—in deference to the young ladies of the manor house, both of the " Bath " and " Garter." *Honi soit qui mal y pense!*

> For her young master, the old African countess preserves an unfailing attachment and a jealous care. All his goings on are criticized with a watchful supervision. . . .Beautiful and touching is the love of these old women for the children they have nursed; and they cherish and love, and scold and forgive them, with the earnestness of real maternity.[23]

---

[21] *Virginia Comedians,* ii, 102.
[22] Ibid., i, 18.
[23] *Henry St. John, Gentleman,* 83.

If to this be added the account of the exalted coachman, Cato, one has, perhaps, the best of which Cooke was capable:

> Old Cato, in a measured and deliberate way, abandoned the horses and approached his master. The colonel, however, desired that Cato should rush rapidly toward him, and the deliberate pace of the old negro caused him to flourish his cane and swear.
>
> Cato did not hasten his steps, however. He seemed to think that he as well as his master had rights, and moreover, was convinced from long experience that the cane would not descend on his shoulders. The event proved his good sense— he preserved his personal dignity and lost nothing.
>
> " Look at the old dog," said the colonel; " he presumes upon my good nature and takes his time. Come, you abandoned old wretch! There! take care of the foot! easy!"
>
> And leaning upon Cato, the old gentleman reached the chariot, and was comfortably deposited within upon the soft cushions. The young girls bade him good-bye, with a kiss; and old Cato having received an intimation from the colonel that he would thrash him on his return, if he drove faster than a slow walk, the chariot rolled away over the smooth gravel at a brisk trot, and was soon out of sight.[24]

Exaggerated, lightly presented, the passage suggests that the author regarded only the comical aspect of the African character. At any rate he was most spirited when making the negro grossly humorous—in such scenes as the one above or others, in *The Virginia Comedians* (1854), recording the antics of " Mr. Crow," whose prototype was the black-faced minstrel, not the flesh-and-blood slave of the plantation.

For characters from actual life, in fact, Cooke ordinarily had little use, so that, after all, the chief reason for his superficial presentation of the negro is found in the kind of fiction he wrote— not realism, but a highly sentimental and idealized romance, concerned almost exclusively with the lives of Southern whites. To such fiction the humble slave could belong only incidentally. At most he could only stand as foil to a meteoric white hero, or play the buffoon. The sparkling dialogues, the brilliant repartee of spirited aristocrats, the vicissitudes of proud families, the fortunes of coquettish and beautiful belles and daring gallants, the de-

---

24 Ibid., 66-7.

lightful refinement of Virginia manners—in short, the whole gaiety and vigor and originality of Southern society under a slaveholding regime—these were the themes Cooke held worthy his pen. Like Page he threw the halo of romance over Virginia plantation life, but unlike him he neglected the part which made all the rest possible —the foundation upon which all this dazzling structure of society was built—the slave.

IX

The quantity of pre-War writings portraying the negro is more significant than the quality. Often he was presented, though seldom with insight, and never with absolute thoroughness—in a well-rounded, lifelike guise. No one pointed out with mastery his little reactions to the commonplace things around him, his whimsicalities and peculiar tastes, exactly what he did or said in those everyday moments when out of the restraining presence of his master; no one presented convincingly his whimsical turns of expression, his inimitable primitive philosophy. Authors who seemingly could have done this did not, and reformers, whose interest was strong, were incapable of sufficient detachment of mind and lacked the artist's purpose. The one made of the negro a useful puppet, at times a hero of secondary importance, frequently a buffoon highly amusing; the other described him as a whining philosopher or at best a sentimental Christian wearing his chains like a martyr.

All these faults of characterization belong to an age of fiction far cruder than our own. Only when the dialect writers of the seventies ushered in a more realistic fiction did the negro—or his typal colleagues, the Pike, the mountaineer, the "cracker," or the Creole—have a fair trial before the great tribunal of novel-readers. But long before, in the multitude of Abolitionist novels, romances of plantation society, antislavery poems, slave narratives which characterized the forties and fifties, he had become familiar to the American public. When, about 1870, Irwin Russell and his followers appeared on the literary horizon, with negro balladry and realistic sketches, they described for their readers no new figure, but rather one already long known—a figure who had, even in their grandfather's day, grinned down from the minstrel platform, who had already stalked, puppet-like, through the scenes of many a conventional romance of Southern life, who had sighed and ranted and prayed in the pages of countless reformers, and who, through it all, occasionally appeared lifelike in brief superior scenes, but who now, at last, had thrown aside the mask completely and stepped forth in his own proper and likable person.

CHAPTER IV

THE SENTIMENTAL HERO IN CHAINS: THE NEGRO
IN ANTISLAVERY VERSE

It now becomes necessary to turn aside and consider, in this and the two chapters which follow, the treatment of the negro character recorded in the effusions of antislavery versifiers, in the slave narratives, and finally in fully developed slavery fiction. As previously pointed out, this treatment was largely independent of that of our literary men, and was more serious, more impassioned, and on the whole farther from reality. First, then, the concept found in antislavery verse.

Perhaps in no way was the spirit of the French Revolution more clearly reflected than in the growth of antislavery sentiment which, logically enough, accompanied the general humanitarian movement. Even before the Revolution, sympathy for the African slave had grown to be general in Europe; after 1800 this feeling was intensified, and for one thing was responsible for a vast quantity of writings in France, in England, in Germany, and in America. Among the earliest forms these writings took was verse—mostly mere sentimental rant, the effusions of men more to be commended for goodness of heart than for poetic fire or hard common sense. Once given a chance, however, this antislavery verse seemed effective propaganda, so that reformers seized upon it gladly, and began to elicit sympathy for the slave by setting forth what manner of man he was—how intelligent, noble, brave, in short inherently worthy.

Again the British were ahead of us—our leaders, first, and later our confederates in reform. Through a long antislavery campaign waged in the British Isles, in which wrought such workers as Cowper and Wordsworth, Englishmen grew to be veterans; later, after their victory in 1832, with the complete expulsion of slavery from the Empire, they turned to aid the Abolitionists in the United States. Americans were considerably influenced by these British co-workers, but in no way more conspicuously than in their writings.

As early as 1680, one Morgan Godwyn published in London *The Negro's and the Indian's Advocate,* a prose tract, in which he pleaded that these races be admitted into the church and also be accorded better treatment. From the middle of the next century onward, and increasing in volume as the years passed, discussion of slavery throve lustily, most of it in prose, but after 1775 some also in verse.   Poetasters like the Rev. J. Jamieson,[1] Captain Marjoribanks,[2] and the Falconar sisters,[3] as well as genuine poets like Cowper, all made contributions.   At first these versifiers were satisfied in attacking merely the slave trade, but this led them speedily to strike at the institution of slavery itself.

The Rev. J. Jamieson, for instance, is moved principally by the inhumanity of tearing Africans from home and friends, but incidentally he condemns the ownership of captives thus taken.   Explaining why he chose verse in which to deliver his message, he announces in a prefatory note: " The principal design of the author hath been to represent simple historical facts in the language of poetry; as this might attract the attention of some who would not otherwise give themselves the trouble of looking into the subject." He then addresses the ladies of England as

> Ye British fair, whose gentle bosoms heave
> The sigh of pity at the tale of woe,

after which, becoming truly declamatory, he condemns the slave trade, and slavery, as wicked and horrible.

The Dying Negro, written in 1773 by Thomas Day and John Bicknell, two Englishmen, presents a striking interpretation of slave character.   In the frontispiece to this book stands a stalwart negro man, a regal-looking creature, whom we see at once to be intended for a hero.   Alone on the upper deck of a slave ship, stripped of all clothing except a girdle and headband, long chains binding together his hands and feet, his bulging muscles rounding out a frame of Apollo-like perfection, with one hand raised to heaven, the other holding a dagger, he looks with determined eyes out upon the gloomy sea.   His face—an impressive one, with full forehead, clearcut, well formed features, and the nobleness of mein suggesting an Othello—expresses a decision which we learn of later, namely that he will not be carried anew into slavery.   At least death is left as an alternative!   Resolved upon dying, he nevertheless clings to life

---

[1] *The Sorrows of Slavery, A Poem.* London, 1789.

[2] *Slavery: An Essay in Verse.* Edinburgh, 1792.

[3] *Poems on Slavery,* by Maria and Harriet Falconar. London, 1788.

long enough to write his betrothed—a white woman, by the way—
the impassioned letter which comprises the poem. His opening
words indicate the tenor of the whole:

"Arm'd with thy sad last gift—the power to die,
Thy shafts, stern Fortune, now I can defy;
Thy dreadful mercy points at length the shore,
Where all is peace, and men are slaves no more."

Nor will he tamely die: cheered by the hope of revenge, he hurls
defiance at his tormentors, sure that in due season they will be
blasted and damned:

"—Thanks, righteous God;—Revenge will soon be mine;
Yon flashing lightning gave the dreadful sign.
I see the flames of heav'nly anger hurl'd,
I hear your thunders shake a guilty world."

Here, surely, is no African savage speaking, but seemingly some
Grecian warrior—a man with the god-like anger of Achilles.

But such misrepresentations were common. The early American antislavery workers, modelling their writings after the British,
continued them.

A pioneer among these American reformers was Thomas Branagan, ex-pirate, ex-West Indian plantation overseer, ex-sailor on a
slave ship—a restless spirit whom love of adventure lured from his
native Ireland. If we can believe his own story, Branagan was
always thoroughly devout at heart, even in his turbulent early career; and although at last fairly on the road to prosperity in the
West Indies, out of pure love for his fellow men he gave up his
lucrative position there to engage in religious work in the United
States. Especially did he wish to aid the slave against whom he
himself had so sinned. In 1803 he published at Philadelphia *A
Preliminary Essay on the Oppression of the Exiled Sons of Africa,*
a prose tract of nearly three hundred pages, and in 1805 followed
his first venture with the mock epic *Avenia.*[4] This was an ambitious
writing, modelled upon the *Iliad* and written after the manner of
Pope. What, he must have asked, could be more effective in en-
listing sympathy for an enslaved race than celebrating them in a
modern epic? Doubtless the world would weep at their sad story.
Doubtless also the world would in time see their wrongs righted.

---

[4] *Avenia: or, A Tragical Poem, on the Oppression of the Human Species,
and Infringements of the Rights of Man.* In Six Books. Written in Imitation of Homer's *Iliad.* By Thomas Branagan. Philadelphia, 1805.

As he wrote away at *Avenia* Branagan imagined how his lines would be received:

> Methinks I see each sentimental fair,
> With tender sorrow wipe the trickling tear,
> While shame and sorrow thro' their bosoms rush,
> Swell ev'ry vein and spread the burning blush.

Certainly only a " sentimental fair " could be so moved over his long story. Even in its own day one wonders how readers, fond though they were of the heroic couplet, could greatly enjoy the book, especially its last section, a moral and religious dissertation on slavery.

The action in the story begins when the slave traders come to an Africa suspiciously Arcadian in its perfection and pastoral repose. With villainous treachery these whites proceed by fraud and force to secure slaves, surprising " the youths and maidens in their artless jollity." A fierce struggle ensues. For a time the noble "African citizens " hold their own, fighting with conspicuous bravery under one of their leaders named Louverture (after the Haitian chieftain?) ; but in the end the traders conquer, slaughter many of the heroic blacks, and carry off a profitable cargo of them to the West Indies. The reader is asked especially to consider the hard lot of a lovely ebony heroine, Avenia, who

> All beautiful in grief. . . .cries
> For pity, to the Sov'reign of the skies.

The appeal does her little good, apparently, for she loses her husband, is ravished by her master, and is finally compelled to commit suicide by leaping from a high cliff into the sea. Branagan did not mean to say, by thus constructing his story, that God had abandoned the world, but rather that the devil, aided by his lieutenants, the slave traders and slaveholders, had won a temporary victory and must therefore be overthrown.

We cannot feel any reality in all this far-fetched, over-idealized, impossible story. Avenia is no African, nor are her friends and kinsmen. Like the heroes and heroines in the literature Branagan was imitating, they are idealized whites. To fire people to action, the writer could more profitably have erred in another direction— in making the scenes too gruesomely realistic. Although *Avenia* might have brought tears to the eyes of some sentimental lady in a well protected home, it did not arouse determination to act in the hearts of practical men. To do that required an *Uncle Tom's Cabin* or the autobiography of a Frederick Douglass.

After Branagan, many others invoked the Muse to aid in the antislavery campaign.[5] The epic was not again essayed, to be sure, but writers of verse used other and shorter forms. For the first two decades of the nineteenth century there was a lull in antislavery versifying; after that date the production increased and continued steadily until the Civil War. Poetaster and poet alike contributed his bit, so that what was written ranged from such genuine poetry as Longfellow's *Slave in the Dismal Swamp* to verse of such glaring worthlessness as the lines " By a little girl eleven years of age ":

> "Slavery is a bitter draught,"
> With care and sorrow it is fraught,
> Though slavery brings sorrow to the mind,
> Yet the slave "refuge in his God" may find.
>
> He loves as well as white men do,
> His nation and his country too;
> The slave has mind unlike the brute,
> Then cultivate kind nature's fruit.[6]

Anthologies of antislavery verse were published by societies and private individuals;[7] Abolitionist song-books appeared with both jingles and genuine poems set to music;[8] a few antislavery plays were published.[9] As for shorter independent "poems," they were legion. Soliloquies by distressed slave mothers, philosophizings on

---

[5] An indication of the growing humanitarian sentiment is furnished by the poet, Joel Barlow, whose *Vision of Columbus* (1787) glorifies America, with no reference to the blight of slavery. Twenty years later, however, when Barlow expanded his poem into *The Columbiad* (1807), he vehemently denounced the evil and warned his countrymen of its danger. Freneau also wrote antislavery verse.

[6] *Star of Emancipation,* 86.

[7] A complete list of the anthologies cannot be included here. See especially *The North Star* (J. G. Whittier, Ed., Phila., 1840); *The Star of Emancipation* (Boston, 1841); most of all, *The Liberty Bell,* an important series, of which fifteen volumes appeared between 1839 and 1859; and *The Garland of Freedom* (W. Armistead, Ed., London, 1853). Although the latter is thus a British publication, it was got out for distribution in America, was mainly about American slavery, and hence may rightly be considered as belonging to America.

[8] See, for example, *Anti-Slavery Melodies* (Hingham, Mass., 1843) and G. W. Clark's two volumes, *The Liberty Minstrel* (1844) and *The Harp of Freedom* (1856).

[9] Note "The Fugitives" in *The Star of Emancipation,* and Mrs. M. T. S. Putnam's *Tragedy of Errors* (1861) and *Tragedy of Success* (1862).

freedom by noble blacks of both sexes, expressions of thanksgiving put into the mouths of escaped fugitives, narratives of slave life— all were cast into poetic form by aroused humanitarians. Before the publications ceased, Bryant, Lowell, Whitman, Longfellow, and Whittier had been drawn in to assist; among the poetasters the ablest were William Lloyd Garrison, William H. Burleigh, John Pierpont, Elizabeth Margaret Chandler, Maria Lowell, and Mrs. Stowe. In addition, much British verse was reprinted, especially that of Cowper. All told, there was a veritable flood of such writing, although little of any decided literary merit.

To understand just how unrepresentative of the truth was most of this antislavery verse, one has only to examine, say, Longfellow's *Slave's Dream,* which if popularity counts for anything ought surely to be placed among the few good poems resulting from American Abolitionism. There is no denying this to be of true poetic stamp; its pleasing cadence, animation, and imaginative appeal lift it above mere verse. Still, note how inconsistent and false to fact! Longfellow did not know the negro; neither did he have any notion of how Africa looked. To one familiar with life in the South it seems hardly likely that the dreaming slave should have had his "matted hair" buried in the sand, nor does the sentimental picture of this once-king (how often these slaves were kings in Africa!) meeting his "dark-eyed queen" and welcoming the excessive caresses of his affectionate children seem quite what we should expect to find in an uncivilized African home. Neither is it likely that the warrior's bridle-reins should have been "golden chains," and again, how unfounded is the conception that the dreaming slave once lived and ruled "beneath the palm-trees on the plain," when probably the truth was that he came from the African jungles, so unconvincingly described, where at night he heard "the lion roar" and "the river-horse, as he crushed the reeds beside some hidden stream." And yet this poem has proved popular and bids fair to continue so. Longfellow could, of course, do better than this, but he did so only once—in *The Slave in the Dismal Swamp.*

It is a sad commentary on antislavery verse that all of it worth preserving as literature could be quoted here without making this chapter unduly long. On practically all of it is the blight of Abolitionist zeal, which grew out of the desire, not to present the negro realistically, or indeed to present him at all, but to free him: he must be shown every whit as intelligent and capable as his master. Most of it is but ill-disguised propaganda. If to the poems of Longfellow already mentioned, we add two or three others by him, eight or ten by Whittier, and a bare dozen by other Americans, we have all that deserve the name of poetry. Why, then, devote a chapter to the negro character as therein pictured? Simply because most of these Abolitionist effusions were attempts at literature; taken as a whole, the verse presented, however distortedly, the negro character to a large part of the American people; and not least, through sheer excess and extravagance, it affected later concepts of African traits and mode of living. To judge antislavery verse without considering the end it was intended to serve would, of course, be unfair; still for purposes of this study, some attention must be accorded the specific errors or misconceptions it helped to propagate.

In brief, the Africans of the Abolitionist poet were little more than white men with black skins—creatures devised by the versifiers, as Professor Wendell has it, in "the simple process of daubing their own faces with burnt cork."[10]   Not only were they assigned the psychology of the white man, but worse still, the psychology of a highly glorified white man. Although objections have been made to drawing distinctions between the negro and the European, undeniably there are wide differences between them. Men belonging to branches of the same race differ noticeably, and how much more men of separate races. Thus when we find the slave, here, always deporting himself as the white man writing of him might under the same circumstances, we must not only pronounce the presentation inaccurate, but in addition deplore its subsequent influence upon fiction.

To proceed to more specific criticism, the negro of antislavery verse speaks a language wholly beyond him both in substance and manner. His diction is poetical, affected; he uses grammar like a scholar; he reasons like a philosopher. And yet, so the Abolitionist contended, his soul has been crushed out by wretched living and unremitting drudgery, and he has been denied all opportunity to develop. If this be true, then, how can we imagine him soliloquizing on liberty as might a man with years of European training and culture behind him—least of all, in an idiom peculiarly the Briton's?

---

[10] *Literary History of America*, 388.

How likely is Whittier's *Farewell* to seem ridiculous if the reader try to imagine the old, ignorant slave mother actually saying, as a steady refrain, " Oh, *woe is me,* my stolen daughters! " It is only fair to note, however, that occasional poems are simple in sentence structure and meaning—were deliberately made so—and that elementary dialect is here and again employed to give verisimilitude. So much for the diction.

The slaves of antislavery verse usually appear brave, noble, capable of great sacrifice, displaying a depth of feeling rare in men of any race. Situations like the following are frequent themes with the antislavery versifiers. A slave father is soliloquizing over the dead body of an infant son:

> 'Tis well! Thou wilt not share those storms with me,
> That is my all of comfort in this hour—
> I weep not, though I would have died for thee!
> Ay, more than died—*that* sacrifice were poor—
> I would have spurned the hand that set me free,
> And clasp'd my chains, and lived a slave for thee.[11]

If this man had been described, he doubtless would have been shown in tattered rags and perhaps manacled as well—a being steeped in misery and wretchedness. Where, one is inclined to ask, did he get his fine sentiments, not to mention the excellent grammar?

The Abolitionist's hero is brave also; he welcomes death as a release from misery:

> Come, kind death! and give me rest,
> Yamba has no friend but thee.[12]

As a matter of fact, in his undeveloped condition, with little chance to call into play any finer sensibilities, the ordinary slave thought more of respite from toil or a good dinner than of seeking the philosopher's sweet solace of death.[13] Yet how often is he made to turn Hamlet and question whether "to be or not to be."

Again, the Abolitionist misunderstood the negro's religion. Undoubtedly the negro was, and still is, religious by nature, but not in the spirit and manner of the white man. It has been said that with the negro even the Christian religion is largely a mat-

---

11 Elizabeth Chandler: *Poems,* 140.
12 *Garland of Freedom,* iii, 100.
13 Slaves sometimes took their lives, because of the hardships of slavery—but never, so far as the present writer knows, because of a reasoned conviction that death was preferable to bondage.

ter of pure emotion, of appeal to his sense of rhythm and of beauty
rather than to his intellect. At services he sings a great deal, even
demanding that the sermons he hears be chanted or half sung; he
is attracted more by a beautiful picture of heaven than by the ab-
struse conception of a divine love. His sermons are not naturally
so logical as they are poetical and imaginative; the picturesque in
the Bible attracts him most. He thinks more of the golden gates
and of the cloud banks with snow-white angels flitting past than
of a puzzling Trinity or of such abstractions as duty or law. The
white man is also emotional in his religion, but in a less intense way;
he builds up complicated theologies, tends to reason logically about
divine matters, and in his ceremonies talks more than he sings.
When, therefore, the slave in the poem before us reasons too wisely
on spiritual matters, questioning with sagacious observations the
justice of a disordered universe, his speech strikes one as somewhere radically amiss. In many poems, however, he merely thanks
God for His mercy or calls on Him for aid, so that this criticism
cannot apply indiscriminately.

These oppressed bondsmen are often put before us as highly
cultured and sensitive folk who consider love in the romantic fashion of a Romeo. In an Africa where the noisy Mumbo Jumbo
rules, where a man may have as many wives as he can capture in
war, and where the whole family may go clad as in the balmy days
of Adam and Eve, how preposterous seems a scene like the following. Two innocent lovers have just been made prisoners and are
about to be separated and carried into slavery. The poet is attempt-
ing to tell us how they feel:

> A slave! The ills of earth are numerous—
> Pain, sickness, sorrow, poverty, and wrong,
>
>   . . . .
>
> . . but what are these, or all
> That poetry can image, or the heart
> Of human anguish suffer, to the deep,
> Dark, desolate, immedicable woe
> Of slavery, bound on the soul, for life!

The lovers find it hard to part—these steadfast lovers who might
aptly be called an African Pyramus and Thisbe. Especially is the
youth crushed at their misfortune—

> Such was the grief
> That rent young Ahmed's heart, when round the neck
> Of Zayda, for the last, last time, he threw
> The manly arm, that in the woods had torn
> The tiger's jaw, and saved her from his rage!

No, he will not leave her with this dastardly slave driver! He defies the villain, and for his pains is struck dead at his love's feet. She, poor thing, knows not what to do:

> She stood—but moved not—shrieked not—gazing down
> Into the eyes she loved, until she fell
> Across his bleeding form—heart-broken—dead.[14]

Not often do we find such nonsense as this, but many times we are given glimpses of domestic slave life highly incongruous with what we know either of marriage customs in Africa or of actual slave life in the South.

But worst of all, the African is time and time again made sentimental. Now, in the usual sense of the word, the negro is said rarely to be sentimental; he is usually too completely a child of the present moment for that. No proof exists that the slave spent his nights sobbing on his pillow, moaning that he bore the curse of Canaan. Be it said to the credit of the negro people that they were not so silly. They suffered hardships more patiently and good-humoredly than perhaps any other people could have done. The Abolitionist versifier, however, living in a sentimental age, when tears were much in vogue in polite literature, thought patience less commendable than weeping, so that many a time " the captive's lone tear " begins before the first stanza of a poem is completed.

Yes, this Abolitionist hero wept incessantly, philosophized on every occasion, each day prayed betimes, and was, withal, as far-fetched and unconvincing a figure as ever appeared in books anywhere, in any age.

The misrepresentations by antislavery versifiers did not abate as the years passed; if anything they grew, if not more flagrant, at least commoner, as the Abolitionists became more prolific in their writings, more determined in their fight, and more and more resolved to see in the slave an extraordinary man. Until the third decade of the nineteenth century, a large part of antislavery writ-

---

14 *Freedom's Gift*, 69 ff.

ings was in verse. After this, although the narrative of the fugitive and the novel on slave life rapidly came to predominate, verse was not pushed entirely into the background; much of it was written down to the Civil War.[15]

---

[15] Note that M. R. Markham's *Alcar, the Captive Creole* (1857) is in verse. Except for this fact, the book differs little from many another melodramatic romance of Southern life. It is conventional, exciting, and full of false notions of slave conditions; incidentally, the verse is decidedly weak. On the Southern side, see W. J. Grayson's *Hireling and Slave* (2nd ed., 1855), also in sorry verse.

Chapter V

THE HEROIC FUGITIVE

The negro in antislavery verse was a long-suffering, tearful soul, philosophizing on his wrongs, whining that his fate was bitter and unrelenting—a creature of refined feelings condemned to live in a filthy hovel and cringe before a brutal master. We now come to another and very different concept, that of the slave defiant—of the slave as leaving philosophy to more comfortable folk and taking to his heels. The one was Uncle Tom in a sentimental mood, the other George Harris fleeing northward. The one concept grew out of sentimental theorizing, the other out of fact. Hundreds of slaves did actually escape to free soil, and of these many wrote accounts of their lives, setting forth direful records of their sufferings and wrongs, inveighing against planters, their former masters, describing slave conditions, and most important of all, incidentally characterizing themselves.

Curiously enough, of the many slave autobiographies, or biographies—for they were often " edited " by friends of the slave—all but three or four seem to be forgotten. For this neglect students of literature are easily excusable, because the narratives are seldom works of art; not so the historians, however, whose need is always for just such illuminating documents. Although filled with the most vociferous propaganda, in parts embittered and untrue, even the worst of them record as nothing else does the workaday life of the *ante-bellum* South. A reader soon learns to distinguish, in the large, the true portions from the falsified, and having done so, he finds himself confronted with pictures of slavery as it was; he discovers how both slaves and masters of the old South actually talked, dressed, carried on their occupations, amused themselves—in short, what their social background was, the world in which they moved.

In the two decades preceding the Civil War, the vogue of slave narratives was enormous. As propaganda they won thousands of friends for the Southern bondsmen, and as gripping stories they rivalled contemporary novels, some " far excelling fiction in their touching pathos." Romantic and thrilling, they interested by the sheer horror of their revelations, and they satisfied in the reading public a craving for the sensational. Needless to say, most slave narratives were hopelessly partisan, telling, except by implication, only one side of the story, and grossly overdrawing that, but what mattered far more at the time, they interested readers and won friends for the slaves.

Nothing could more clearly show their popularity than that some of them sold at all, for often they were trivial indeed.   By 1850 practically any writing by or about a negro was in demand, even if he had never been a slave.   The only requisites were a black skin and a grievance.   Destitute blacks of both sexes energetically demanded help from the "charitable reader," who was admonished, in the name of humanity, to buy their books.[1]   Northern negro preachers who had never in their lives set foot on slave soil rushed confidently into print, begging for assistance or extolling their good work.[2]   Ex-slaves like Frederick Douglass, Father Henson, and Sojourner Truth found it profitable to publish more than one story of their experiences.   Northern—sometimes British—" editors " came gladly to the aid of the newly arrived fugitive who wished to write his life history.   Even publishers shared in the general enthusiasm: once at least a publisher imposed on his credulous public by reissuing an old story under a new title.   Twenty-two years after it first appeared, the excellent narrative of Charles Ball was seized upon, condensed slightly, bound in a fiery red cover, with great wavering gilt letters staring out at the reader, and handed out to an eager public under the astonishing title, *Fifty Years in Chains*.   The public was told, moreover, that the slave thus held for fifty years was still alive, and that revealing his name would make him liable to capture—this although his name had been blazoned abroad on title-pages for two decades—and whereas the brief preface intimated quite clearly that this was the first printing of the story, it had gone through at least two editions before.

It is now impossible to ascertain the number of separately published narratives, but a conservative estimate would put it at more

---

[1] See especially *Memoirs of Elleanor Eldridge* (1838), *Elleanor's Second Book* (1839), *A Narrative of the Life and Travels of Mrs. Nancy Prince* (1850—third edition, 1856), *Our Nig* (1859), *Broken Gloom* (1851)—the latter composed of sketches of negroes, written to aid the inmates of the Colored Home of the City of New York.

[2] See *Incidents in the Life of the Rev. J. Asher* (1850), *The Looking-Glass: Being a True . . . Narrative of the Life . . of the Rev. D. H. Peterson* (1854) ; and more readable than either, *The Narrative of the Life of Rev. Noah Davis* (1859). Davis had once been a slave.

than a hundred. This leaves out of account numerous briefer sketches which appeared in *The Liberator* and antislavery anthologies. A number of narratives, too, were published in England by fugitives escaped thither, but these may be counted among our own, for not only were they intended to sell here as in the British Isles, but their subject matter and authors were American. The narratives became common in this country about 1840, then increased steadily in number till the Civil War, after which, naturally enough, few new ones appeared.

When one comes to examine the troop of fugitives here presented, he is struck by the vivid personalities among them and their variation in type. Not a few of these escaped slaves show the negro at his best, with virtues almost peculiar to the race and an intelligence far above that of the usual plantation menial. Such a man was Charles Ball, such was Solomon Northup, such was old Father Henson—the original of Mrs. Stowe's Uncle Tom. Charles Ball's narrative was one of the earliest, as well as one of the most pithy, informative, and unbiased.[3] A slave for years, sold hither and yon, suffering the whip, starvation, insult, and excessive tasking, Ball could yet write of his experiences fairly and without bitterness, and this not through mere servility or obsequiousness, but because of never-failing patience and a forbearance seemingly proof against all misfortune; the whole account is in a straightforward, manly vein. Northup's performance appears still more remarkable —as nothing short of astounding, in fact.[4] This man, a free citizen of New York State, was kidnapped and sold into slavery on the notorious Red River of Louisiana. Here for twelve years he was driven, flogged, and kicked about by brutal planters until rescued by a Northern friend and restored to his family. In spite of this horrible ordeal in the South, however, he still found it possible to recount his misfortunes with fairness and justice—a feat of no small magnitude, and one of which few men, certainly few white men, would be capable. Nor was this calm and unresentful atti-

---

[3] *Slavery in the United States: A Narrative of the Life and Adventures of Charles Ball* (1836). The book went into a second edition in 1837, and in 1858 was republished as *Fifty Years in Chains*. See above, page 61.

[4] *Twelve Years a Slave. Narrative of Solomon Northup, a Citizen of New York* (1853). The work was copiously reprinted. Other narratives to be compared with Ball's and Northup's are *Memoir of Pierre Toussaint* (by Mrs. Hannah F. S. Lee) (1854) and *Twenty-two Years a Slave and Forty Years a Freeman* (1857), by Austin Steward.

tude the result of simplicity, for though possessing the yielding disposition of his race, Northup was nevertheless highly intelligent.
The shrewd observations in the book and Northup's calm estimates
make *Twelve Years a Slave* a superior and unique treatment of
Southern slavery. As a historical document it is worth more than
the charmingly simple and unaffected history of Father Henson,
although Father Henson himself has an appeal all his own.[5] Patient, reliable, without malice, a Christian through and through, he
is today far more appealing than Mrs. Stowe's martyr, and in the
flesh a stronger argument against slavery than mountains of argumentative pamphlets and ethical discourses.

Not all of Henson's brethren were so admirable, however. Upon
some of them Abolitionists showered more attention than was sensible, and unhappily enough spoiled their protégés—of whom a particularly unlovely example was Samuel Ringgold Ward.[6] A fairly
able man living at a time when proof of African intellectual power
was greatly needed, Ward was hailed as a mighty writer, orator,
and thinker; and the praise went to his head quickly and with unfortunate results. In England, where he was feted and feasted
like a Roman hero, he shortly began not only to talk familiarly of
his new friends in the British nobility, but to complain that the
United States still harbored people who would not greet him as
peer and brother. Almost every page he wrote is marred by excessive egotism, so that although his writing is forcible, it has
scarcely any other commendable quality. If Henson and Northup
and Ball did their race honor, Ward disgraced it—but he would
have been a disgrace to any race.

Usually, however, it was not egotism, nor self-importance, nor
pomposity, nor over-sophistication, that characterized the fugitive,
but rather bitterness and wild-eyed indignation. Suffering every
humiliation of bondage, often driven into flight through cruelty,
what was more natural than that the fugitive should bitterly arraign
his former master? What slave of any race would not have done

---

[5] *The Life of Josiah Henson, Formerly a Slave, Now an Inhabitant of
Canada*—As Narrated by Himself (1849). Henson himself wrote the account
later. See *Father Henson's Story of His Own Life* (1858).

[6] *Autobiography of a Fugitive Negro* (1855), by S. G. Ward. Ward had
never been a slave; he was a " fugitive " from justice in the United States.
Other accounts of rascally negroes are *Slave Life in Georgia: A Narrative of
. . . . John Brown, A Fugitive Slave, Now in England* (1855), *The Life of
John Thompson, A Fugitive Slave* (1856), and *The Story of the Life of John
Anderson* (1863).

so? It is significant, however, that just as the most restrained accounts, the fairest in tone, were from pure-blooded Africans, so the bitterest, the most overdrawn ones came from mulattoes or men of more white blood still. Typical of this class was Frederick Douglass, a notable antislavery leader and an orator known on two continents, and William Wells Brown, also a successful orator, writer, and Abolitionist campaigner. Douglass's well written narrative, grossly unfair to Southern life and people, is yet highly meaningful in showing how an intelligent man—a man whose mental constitution was Anglo-Saxon, whose will was the white man's also—how such a man reacted to being classed as another man's property.[7] Brown was likewise more white than negro, but his narrative is fairer in tone, less impassioned, less bitter; in his capacity as plantation waiter, house servant, henchman of a slave trader, he saw more of slavery, but suffered less from its cruelty than Douglass.[8]

Bitterest and most vindictive of all the fugitives, perhaps, was Lewis Clarke, again largely white and again a long and pitiful sufferer.[9] After his escape from "captivity" in Kentucky, he assailed the whole South with indiscriminate hatred, apparently wishing his audiences to believe the whole region a veritable hell, and the slaveholders who overran it devils who lived only to torment their victims with lash and stake. A few extracts will sufficiently illustrate his method and temper:

> ...I have seen Mrs. B. [a slaveholder], with a large knife drawn in her right hand, the other upon the collar of her husband, swearing and threatening to cut him *square in two*. They both drank freely, and swore like highwaymen. He was a gambler and counterfeiter. I have seen and handled his moulds and false coins.
> ... [She had] her peculiar contrivance for keeping us awake. She would sometimes sit, by the hour, with a dipper of vinegar and salt, and throw it in my eyes to keep them open. My hair was pulled until there was no longer any pain from that source.
> ... The enraged master put a handful of nail-rods into the fire,

---

[7] *Narrative of the Life of Frederick Douglass* (1845); Douglass subsequently wrote several enlarged accounts of his life.

[8] *Narrative of William Wells Brown, A Fugitive Slave* (1847); Brown also wrote other histories of himself.

[9] *Narratives of the Sufferings of Lewis and Milton Clarke . . . among the Slaveholders of Kentucky* (1845). Cf. *The Narrative of the Life and Adventures of Henry Bibb, An American Slave* (1849).

and when they were *red-hot,* took them out, and cooled one after another of them in the blood and flesh of the poor slave's back.

Such unfairness as this must have failed of some of its effect even on Abolitionists; but the book was exciting, and most important of all, gave the reader a conception—for the most part, a false one—of what manner of man the plantation owner held enslaved.

Practically all of the slave narratives set negro psychology and personality before the public in an unusual light. Being autobiographies, or supposed autobiographies, they of course presented real men, whose names were given, whose owners were specified, whose histories were detailed, but men somewhat unrepresentative of the great mass of slaves left undisturbed behind, at work in the cotton fields. Ordinarily only the ablest, the shrewdest, in other words, the most exceptional, of the slaves made their way north; and again, many of the successful fugitives were scarcely negroes at all, but men European in mental heritage, in emotional quality, in spirit and temper. For illustration, one has but to recall Douglass, Brown, Henry Bibb, the Clarke brothers, none of whom was quite representative of the happy-go-lucky, ignorant, coon-hunting, fun-loving field hand who, more than any other class of slave, typified the great mass of black men throughout the South.

But even if these fugitives had been representative, their accounts would still be untrustworthy reflections of their characteristics and lives, for generally escaped negroes were not allowed to write unassisted. Abolitionist editors soon seized upon their stories as propaganda and cast them into the form calculated to horrify a too complacent North, closely supervising the trend of the narrative, making light of incidents which suggested that some master was kind, or a slave unworthy, or a Southern minister Christian at heart, or an overseer human. Not only this, but the editors frequently made additions all their own, rounding out the action, filling in the background, bringing in as minor characters the fellow slaves of the hero under consideration—resorting to anything, in short, which made the writing more readable and hence better propaganda. The additions ranged from details not furnished by the slave to fully elaborated plots and troops of characters. Before committing his book to press, the unknown editor of *The Rev. J. W. Loguen, as a Slave and as a Freeman* (1859) candidly admitted having " occasionally supplied vacancies from [Loguen's] southern life " from fancy. Except as testimony of his honesty, the admission is superfluous, for without it we could see what had been done. Such editorial improvement is evident, also, in many other narratives—in *The Life and Opinions of Julius Melbourn* (1847), *The Kidnapped and the Ransomed* (1856), *Running a Thousand Miles for Freedom* (1860), and *Incidents in the Life of a Slave Girl* (1861), all of which, while based on facts, depend for their interest chiefly upon evident fabrications.

This last work, edited by the story-writer Mrs. Child and suspiciously like a sentimental novel, suggests that there was, in fact, another group of these books not genuine narratives at all, but wholly fictitious—romances masquerading as authentic autobiographies—a group related, on the one hand, to antislavery verse and on the other to antislavery fiction. In narratives of this class the hero is usually sentimental, super-refined in manner and feeling, more like the philosophizing slave of the versifiers than the red-blooded fugitive of real life. On the other hand, this hero has also an affinity with Uncle Tom, in that both are purely fictional creations and both heroes of elaborate stories.

Earliest of the forged narratives was *The Slave: or the Memoirs of Archy Moore,* published first in 1836, and mistaken by many at the time for what it purported to be. The book is artificial in sentiment and devoid of convincing descriptions; comparing it with, say, the narrative of Lewis Clarke, one can readily see the difference between the two types. With all its hollowness, however, *Archy Moore* was reprinted many times by the Abolitionists, who persisted in believing it despite the somewhat tardy admission by Hildreth the historian that he was the "author."

In 1847 there was published in London *The Life and Adventures of Zamba, an African King; and His Experiences of Slavery in South Carolina,* in some ways the most successful—certainly the most readable—of the fictitious narratives. The book contains sweep of action and a background striking enough to hold the attention of readers. Zamba (so the story goes) was brought up in Africa, the son and heir of Zembola, king of a small principality on the river Congo, and at an early age, after the death of his father, begins to rule. Doubtless he would long have continued on the throne but for a restlessness and an ambition somewhat unfortunate: he longs to know what lies beyond the seas—longs so persistently that when a slave trader, to whom he often sells slaves without knowing the enormity of his crime, offers to conduct him thither, he gladly accepts the invitation. The trader, a rascal of darkest hue, betrays the royal guest, throws him into chains, and with poor business judgment—considering the usefulness of the king as a source of supply—sells him on the Charleston slave market. By chance Zamba falls into the hands of a kind master, discovers by accident one day his wife, Zillah, on the slave block and persuades his master to buy her, eventually purchases his own freedom, becomes a Christian, and settles happily in Charleston, with no thought of returning to the Congo. His enslaved countrymen around him, however, are not so fortunate, and to help them he writes his history, hoping, he says, to reveal the workings of slavery as exemplified in his own life. From the declaration of such a purpose we should naturally expect heated arguments against slavery, bitter denunciation, the evident zeal of a sufferer fighting the good fight; but actually the little antislavery discussion there is, all in the last few chapters, is weak and tame, and appears to have been added as an afterthought, to carry out the avowed purpose of the volume. The story was the chief concern of the author, as it is ours. Apparently some author (Peter Neilson, the editor?), seeing the widespread interest in Abolition, and remembering *Oroonoko,* sought to exploit African life and the slave while demand made the undertaking profitable. Mrs. Behn's story and *Zamba* resemble each other in several particulars: the heroes are both kings betrayed by rascally slave traders, the scenes in the African principalities are somewhat alike, both books contain romantic love stories, and have, as a chief interest, not the problem of slavery so much as the sight of royalty fallen to low estate. Even the difference that *Oroonoko* ends tragically and *Zamba* happily is but superficial.

One other example of the fictitious slave narrative will perhaps suffice—*The Autobiography of a Female Slave* (1857), which suggests the narrative only in title. No convincing proof is offered that the book deals with fact; the names of places in the story are not spelled in full; there is an elaborate plot, with climax and abundant subaction; a conspicuous effort at literary finish is discernible—all evidences that the book is not the unpretentious record of truth it purports to be. Moreover, the author was considerably influenced by *Uncle Tom's Cabin.* Except for his sex John Peterkin is another little Eva: he has the same excessively precocious and angelic nature; he talks in the same wise and prophetic strain; and he, also, fades away and dies, a flower too good for this wicked and slavery-cursed world. Everywhere there is an abundance of sentimentality —much weeping, sighing, poetizing, affected expression of feeling. Even the slaves are sentimental, especially the almost white heroine, who speaks of watering the lovely flowers with her tears, as though this were nothing out of the ordinary, and who preserves, as her chief and dearest treasure, the note her lover wrote before killing himself to escape slavery. Of this note she writes:

> ... Lying beside me now, dear, sympathetic reader, is *that note —his last brief words.* Before writing this chapter [which is called "The Crisis of Existence—A Dreadful Page in Life"] I read it over. Old, soiled and worn it is; but by his trembling fingers those blotted and irregular lines were penned; and to me they are precious, though they awaken ten thousand bitter emotions! I look at the note but once a year, and then on the fatal anniversary, which occurs to-day! I have pressed it to my heart, and hearsed it away, not to be reopened for another year.

Such sentimentality belongs only to slaves existing, or once existing, in the over-drawn and dreary pages of Abolitionist romancers.

The Autobiography of a Female Slave was, in fact, but a feeble imitation of *Uncle Tom's Cabin,* and whereas *Archy Moore* and *Zamba* suggest how slave narratives led naturally to fiction, this book illustrates how, after the appearance of Mrs. Stowe's work, fiction overshadowed all other forms of Abolitionist writings.

Chapter VI

UNCLE TOM AND HIS COMPEERS

A. *Introductory*

The antislavery novel was a natural development from the earlier accounts of slave life in verse and prose. From both sources it borrowed much—from the verse, a sentimental attitude toward the slave, the assumption that he was unhappy on philosophical grounds, because of the humiliation attaching to his lowly condition; from the prose, those gruesome, realistic scenes showing brutal planters, filthy living quarters, violent cruelty and wretchedness everywhere on the plantations. In brief, the antislavery novel effectively combined the sentimental appeal made in the verse and the shocking accusations of the prose. That is, the later fiction did this; the earliest specimens, however, were often puerile and crude. Of such a stamp were most of the prose pieces in Mrs. Lydia Maria Child's *Oasis* (1834), *The North Star* (1840), and *The Liberty Bell* (an annual beginning in 1839), miscellanies which contained not only antislavery verse, but prose stories as well, many of them fictitious. Less crude and more important was the fictitious slave narrative, which, as has already been seen, began in 1836 with *Archy Moore*. Slave narratives, in fact—both the true and the fictitious—mightily affected the fiction; preceding it, furnishing the material out of which many a second-hand account of Southern life was elaborated, and although themselves influenced in turn by the fiction, leading directly to *Uncle Tom's Cabin* and other such books. Not Mrs. Stowe alone but all the Abolitionist novelists were indebted to them as sources of influence.

The slave narratives were supplemented by other fountainheads of information on slave life, prominent among which were accounts of foreign visitors to the United States. Although the earliest of these appeared before the fiction, they rode to popularity on the wave of interest set moving by the fiction, and as this grew greater, the books of travel became more numerous. Martineau's *Society in America* (1837) and Tocqueville's *Democracy in America* (1838)[1] were especially popular, and their hurried analysis of our society, especially that of the former, went far towards misinforming the

---

[1] The French original was published in 1835.

world at large on American conditions. Others by Sturge, Pulszky, Murray, Trollope, and Reid were also widely read.[2] Although a few visitors took sides with the South, most of them condemned slavery; and again, although some were fair-minded in their opposition, most denounced indiscriminately every feature of the institution. Portions of the travel-books were like fiction in that they dealt in detail with Southern life, especially with planters and their slaves, and like fiction they were read mainly for enjoyment, unfolding before the eyes of the world a fascinating social panorama. Nothing could more clearly show this kinship with fiction that that at least once a half-way novel appeared in the mask of a traveller's account. *Shahmah in Pursuit of Freedom* (1858), professedly the journal of an Algerian's travels in this country, is in all likelihood fictitious both as to the travels and the traveller—an argumentative production, with an elaborate maze of melodramatic happenings, all designed to show how grieved and disappointed was this idealistic pilgrim at finding the institution of slavery thriving in the " land of the free and the home of the brave."

Even more closely allied to fiction than the accounts by foreigners were those of Northern visitors to the South. Apparently some of these volumes were written because the Abolitionist romancers needed support—were designed, as it were, to second the antislavery novels, to give the stamp of authority to the almost incredible pictures drawn by the novelists. They ranged from Olmsted's fair, accurate, comprehensive descriptions to Parsons's vindictive and partisan *Inside View of Slavery* (1855).[3] Often the traveller dealt

---

[2] The most nearly complete bibliography of these foreign accounts is found in *The Cambridge History of American Literature.* Books recording experiences in Africa were also forthcoming occasionally. At least one of them—*Captain Canot, or Twenty Years of an African Slaver* (1854)—is remarkable in containing a calm, matter-of-fact discussion of the cruelties of those engaged in supplying the American slave markets with their human merchandise.

[3] Olmsted's books are: *A Journey Through Texas* (1857), *A Journey in the Seaboard Slave States* (1856), *A Journey in the Back Country* (1860). Fair in tone, and pleasantly written, these volumes were designed to set forth the true state of affairs in the South, and through a non-partisan stand bring the two sections together. They are invaluable as historical material. Contrast them not only with Parsons's *Inside View* but also with Tower's *Slavery Unmasked* (1856) and Redpath's *Roving Editor* (1859). Although not published until 1863, Fanny Kemble's *Journal of a Residence on a Georgia Plantation in 1838-9* belongs here in the list. Bitter, forcibly written, filled with arresting falsehoods, it was widely read and has continued to receive more credence than it deserves.

with negroes, interviewing them, describing their appearance and
actions, discussing them as a great problem. A strain of fiction is
quite evident in some of these impulsively written pages, even when
the account is based on an actual journey. But by no means were
all such accounts based on actual journeys.[4]

But after all, it is with the fiction proper that we are mainly
concerned. More vociferously than the antislavery verse or the
slave narrative, this fiction professed to set forth the real negro,
drawn from life.

In one sense, Mrs. Stowe may be said to have provoked the
deluge of both antislavery and proslavery novels. After her there
arose a school of Abolitionist romancers to dilate upon other suffering Uncle Toms and tiger-hearted Legrees; after her, too, arose a
group of Southern writers to deny the existence in real life of such
monstrosities and to proclaim loudly that the negro was fortunate
in bondage. The South answered Mrs. Stowe with a volley of
novels calculated to make her out an unblushing and malicious liar.
As the fifties passed and the struggle grew fiercer, antislavery activities aroused to a blind fury both North and South. Instead of
the mild antislavery feeling of Cooper's *Spy* we now find the flam-
ing partisanship of *The Planter's Victim* (1855), a book of un-
relieved and unmitigated horrors. On the Southern side, along
with the sunny sketches of the school of Kennedy and Hungerford
and the conventional Southern romances of Simms and Mrs.
Holmes, we find the fierce charges of Fitzhugh's *Cannibals All; or
Slaves Without Masters* (1857), in which it was held that in civi-
lized society nearly all men are slaves, the Southern negroes less
crushingly so than most. The Abolitionists called the Southerners
" soul-drivers " and murderers; the Southerners, in turn, called the
Abolitionists robbers of human property and traitors to the Constitution.

Today these novels strike us as amusingly crude. Nowadays
we are usually more subtle in issuing propaganda, so that even our
most earnest problem novels we try, by means of various subter-
fuges, to disguise as art. The writers of the fifties lacked this sub-

---

[4] In this field also were fictitious publications, showing clearly the link with
antislavery romances. For example, note the *Records of an Obscure Man*
(1861), by Mrs. Lowell Putnam. Among other purposes this book served to
advertise the author's plays in verse soon to appear—*The Tragedy of Errors*
(1861) and *The Tragedy of Success* (1862).

tlety, producing novels so obviously biassed that it is difficult to
see how any but partisans could have read them—except perhaps
to guage the enormity of their lies. Their villains were deep-dyed,
their heroes excessively brave and noble. According to Northern
writers, Southerners all carried revolvers, chewed immense quanti-
ties of tobacco, drank undiluted whiskey by the quart, and ignored
grammar completely. On the other hand, Southern champions de-
picted the Abolitionists as fiendish double-dealers, as sallow-faced,
mean-spirited, interfering reformers, who enticed happy slaves away
from their families and friends only to let them starve or freeze
to death on hostile " free soil," or else meet the worse fate of being
slaughtered by the fickle Northern mob.

Least of all did these partisan novelists deem it necessary to supply adequate motives for the actions of their characters. In
Northern fiction, if a man was a planter, it followed mechanically
that he was a soulless rake, the father of a whole tribe of mulatto
children—a Nero among his black subjects. Or, to take the other
side, if a man was an Abolitionist, it followed no less surely that
he was a pernicious agitator, a sickly coward, whose soul danced
with demoniacal joy when a contented slave was lured to Canada
or the North. In the antislavery stories the poor slaves themselves
are for the most part human footballs, for a depraved master to
kick at pleasure; in the proslavery volumes they are the pampered
minions of super-benevolent owners. According to some of the
latter books, the whites apparently existed mainly to support and
indulge their African protégés.

Time and again, both Abolitionist and Southerner repeated favorite themes—themes which had proved effective stock arguments.
How many well meaning fathers put off manumitting their slave
children just a few days too long, with the resulting tragedy! How
frequently debt caused the separation of master and slave! If these
were the gentle themes—as indeed they must be called—there were
others fierce and repelling. Masters rejoiced in selling their own
progeny; with astonishing frequency beautiful quadroon women fell
into the hands of lascivious masters, especially if they were married already or betrothed; overseers took peculiar delight in killing
the ablest and most faithful menial under their charge. To oppose
all this, the Southern group used certain oft-repeated arguments.
Through being enslaved, they contended, the negro had had con-

ferred upon him the greatest of all boons, Christianity. Moreover, he was happier here than in fever-stricken and cannibal Africa— as a matter of fact, happier than the so-called free white laborers of the North and England. And so the battle raged.

In the struggle, the negro character of fiction suffered heavily. He fell victim to the attacks and counter-attacks of both factions, and was so torn between them as to be distorted almost beyond recognition. Seldom was he a normal human being, but a strange creature, a living argument for one party or the other. If Simms and other men of letters had made him serve the mechanical purposes of the story, the writers of this slavery struggle made him serve the purposes of propaganda. Arguments were embodied as characteristics. The antislavery author, undertaking to prove that he was right about slavery, evolved in his pages a character noble, honest, ambitious, either completely crushed or brutalized by the demands of a terrible life, or at best held in the contentment of the benighted. Likewise the proslavery romancer, in his zeal to uphold the opposite side, pictured the slave as contented, too childish to look out for himself and hence in need of a master, and spoiled and unlikable only when contaminated by abominable reformers. On both sides the portrayals were strained and overdrawn.

Into such crude pages, then, only an occasional realistic negro character strayed. Once in a long while a fictional slave might act naturally enough to satisfy the critic, but only for a moment. He had to be about his business of exemplifying proslavery or Abolitionist principles. The number of good single strokes of characterization in these novels is surprisingly great—in small details, indeed, especially in brief dialogues, they not infrequently surpass the romances of Simms and others—but viewed in the large the characterizations are irredeemably artificial.

Since in a sense Mrs. Stowe was responsible for both streams of the fiction, it is proper here to consider her work first, and then pass on to the other antislavery writers, and after that to their opponents, the Southern partisans.

B. *Mrs. Stowe*

Uncle Tom!—one of those strange things, a household term! How familiar he seems, and yet really to understand him we must know something of how he came into being—the conditions under which Mrs. Stowe wrote, her aims, her equipment.

Doubtless no other novel has had such a remarkable history or has affected so noticeably the life of a nation as *Uncle Tom's Cabin*. Perhaps, too, no other novel has caused so much dispute. Opinions of it are many. " In its power of pathos, in its passionate humanitarianism, in its instinctive art, it is unique. It has the rare kind of greatness which belongs to a large and simple design faithfully executed."[5]   Thus writes one critic, who though an admirer of Mrs. Stowe is not hopelessly prejudiced. Others have thought the book wicked, or mendacious, or seditious, or at best wholly worthless. A conservative judge is Professor Pattee, and perhaps most of us in this age would agree with him in his estimate: *"Uncle Tom's Cabin* was written by one. . . who drew her materials largely from her feelings and her imagination, and made instead of a transcript of actual life, a book of religious emotion, a swift, unnatural succession of picturesque scene and incident, an improvisation of lyrical passion—a melodrama."[6]

Mrs. Stowe was eminently fitted to write the book which should set all Christendom ablaze with antislavery sentiment. For many years she met and talked with the escaping fugitives as they passed through Ohio on their way still farther north; she came into intimate contact with leaders of Abolitionism; she was also privileged to know some of the ablest of the negro leaders themselves, and the life histories of others she read.[7]   In the year 1851 Mrs. Stowe understood the negro well enough to make her characterizations of him convincing to a not over-critical public; more important still, she did not know him too well—that is, she knew him too superficially ever to question the sentimental analysis she made of his heart and soul. Moreover, her book was launched at the auspicious moment, and by a happy combination of appropriateness and timeliness was able to turn into one mighty stream the various currents of antislavery feeling, of political animosity against a unified slavery faction, and of widespread humanitarian sentiment. *Uncle Tom* was a part of the age itself, a reflection of its tastes and demands, combining in admirable proportion the sensational and the sentimental. Slave narratives, travellers' accounts, and other books con-

---

[5] W. J. Dawson: *The Makers of Modern Fiction,* 265-6. Quoted from MacLean's *"Uncle Tom's Cabin" in Germany.*

[6] F. L. Pattee: *A History of American Literature since 1870,* 228.

[7] Mrs. Stowe admitted that Father Henson and Lewis Clarke, two fugitives whose stories she knew, furnished her suggestions for Uncle Tom and George Harris respectively.

tained all the information found in Mrs. Stowe's novel, but their material was not so effectively arranged, not so marshalled as best to play upon the well-exercised sentiments of a reading public.

Despite its tremendous influence, however, we of today find little to admire in *Uncle Tom's Cabin,* at least as a work of art. It is technically faulty, crudely didactic, and anything but a true reflection of life. Although realistic in spots, it is not true to local scene and character. Its effective scenes succeed because of the sentiment behind them, not because they are convincing accounts of what once actually happened upon a particular Southern plantation.

The novel is comprehensive in that it treats the whole matter of negro slavery by personifying the forces at work. Doubtless Mrs. Stowe did not intend to personify anything; doubtless her readers did not realize she had done so. Nevertheless, Simon Legree is not a man, nor yet a brute, so much as he is the personification of the evil of slavery; little Eva is no normal child, nor a child at all, but rather a personification of the good in the master class protesting against slavery. Even Uncle Tom himself, human though he seems at rare moments, is no realistic negro, but a personification of the slave in noble protest against degradation. Almost every character serves a didactic purpose; each is an embodied Abolitionist theory. Even the almost realistic Topsy evidently illustrates the belief that there is no slave, however irresponsible and frivolous, who cannot be redeemed through love. Other arguments, evident at a glance, are incorporated in Madame St. Clare, Miss Ophelia, Eliza, and George Shelby.

An examination of Mrs. Stowe's slave characters shows them to be, strictly speaking, no negroes at all, but a kind of hybrid folk, drawn partly from her imagination, and partly from the observation of negro servants in her own household. In the main, principal characters like Uncle Tom, George Harris, and Eliza are primarily creatures of her fancy; in the main, too, her minor ones like Topsy and Sam are sketched largely from observation. Yet the latter are not based firmly enough on truth to be representative. Mrs. Stowe could not long keep her negro consistent. He was endowed, not only with traits which run true to form, but in addition with Anglo-Saxon sentiment and a Gallic fondness for expressing emotion through physical action: he showed grief or despair by periodically lifting his hands or gazing heavenward—actions habitual with the negro only in the imaginations of Abolitionists, or in the wood-cuts of their publications, never in real life. Certainly in real life no negro talked like Uncle Tom or Aunt Chloe, whose phraseology is full of inconsistencies and false notes, realistic in spots but unsustained. In one scene Legree says to Tom:

> ". . .Come, Tom, don't you think you'd better be reasonable?—heave that ar old pack of trash [the Bible] in the fire, and join my church!"
> "The Lord forbid!" said Tom fervently.

Again, consider the famous scene of the death of Uncle Tom:

> When George [Shelby] entered the shed, he felt his head giddy and his heart sick.
> "Is it possible—is it possible?" said he, kneeling down by him. "Uncle Tom, my poor, poor old friend!"
> Something in the voice penetrated to the ear of the dying. He moved his head gently, smiled, and said,—
> "Jesus can make a dying bed
> Feel soft as downy pillows are."
> Tears which did honor to his manly heart fell from the young man's eyes, as he bent over his poor friend.
> "Oh, dear Uncle Tom! do wake—do speak once more! Look up! Here's Mas'r George,—your own little Mas'r George. Don't you know me?"
> "Mas'r George!" said Tom, opening his eyes, and speaking in a feeble voice. "Mas'r George!" He looked bewildered.
> Slowly the idea seemed to fill his soul; and the vacant eye became fixed and brightened, the whole face lighted up, the hard hands clasped, and tears ran down his cheeks.
> "Bless the Lord! it is,—it is,—it's all I wanted! They haven't forgot me. It warms my soul; it does my old heart good! Now I shall die content! Bless the Lord, oh, my soul!"

There is nothing realistic about this, nothing to suggest the African in the dying man; but sentimentality it has in abundance, and it was this sentimentality that the author substituted for realism. In her generous distribution of it, even poor Topsy failed to escape:

> Topsy made a short courtesy, and looked down; and, as she turned away, Eva saw a tear roll down her dark cheek.

On the other hand, and partly redeeming her portrayal of the African, Mrs. Stowe showed occasional flashes of understanding. Sometimes scraps of dialect are passable—expressions like "dat's what I wants to know," " dis yer time," and " o' that ar '." Some few whole speeches are convincing enough to escape censure. An old negress fears she is about to be sold away from her son:

"Dey needn't call me worn out yet," said she, lifting her shaking hands. "I can cook yet, and scrub, and scour,—I'm wuth a buying, if I do come cheap;—tell 'em dar ar,—you *tell* 'em," she added earnestly.

These good scenes are usually brief, however. Few of the long scenes are better than, say, the not altogether successful account of the exploits of Dinah in the St. Clare kitchen, an account exaggerated and over-comic, but yet fundamentally sound. Dinah, toned down a bit, would seem at least passably real.

Unfortunately we cannot say the same of the hero of the book. Unquestionably Mrs. Stowe visualized Uncle Tom—that we cannot doubt—but just as unquestionably no such gentle soul ever existed on a real plantation. He is a hybrid, the product resulting when Mrs. Stowe's theories about the negro were engrafted on her somewhat slender store of fact. Although of course more lifelike than W. S. Gilbert's impossible folk, and of a very different stamp, he can be said to be characterized only in the sense that they are. Genuinely noble at heart, he exhibits most of humanity's virtues and none of its vices. Faithful, patient, forgiving, religious almost to the point of sainthood, he appears altogether too good to be human—and is, in fact, an artificial hero who in an age of artificial romance and fanatical Abolitionism passed for the epitome of all African virtues. This, in a way, explains the greatness of the character. From one point of view, Uncle Tom is greater than if he had been real—he is the embodiment of a great idea, an ideal, however false.

The other negro heroes of the book need not detain us. George Harris and Eliza are too nearly white to be of moment here. Mrs. Stowe admitted that Harris was suggested by the fugitive Lewis Clarke, whose looks scarcely hinted at an African taint, so nearly white was he. Incidentally there is this difference between the two men: whereas Lewis Clarke was a spiteful, mean-spirited, revengeful man, George Harris is noble, brave, generous. Neither George nor Eliza was a faithful reproduction of any African prototype.

Mrs. Stowe's second novel, *Dred,* is more gruesome and gloomy, but a more powerfully written book than *Uncle Tom.* Its pages are pervaded by the haunting mysticism of the hero; and despite its sentimentality, its crudeness in motivation, and its artificially designed plot, *Dred* frequently gets hold of the reader, grips his attention and forces him to continue.

Purposing to show " the general effect of slavery on society "—or, more specifically, its disastrous effect on the master class—Mrs. Stowe resorted to the cut and dried methods of her earlier work, in fact, repeating much from that earlier work. Like George and Eliza, Harry and his wife are almost white. Tom Gordon is another Legree—in some ways more abominable. The sagely waggish little Tomtit suggests Topsy; the negroes are so over-indulged as to remind one of the pampered members of the St. Clare household. Moreover, there is the same evident aim to show at once the attractive and the tragic side of slave life by going to extremes both ways.

In this book Mrs. Stowe showed no clearer understanding of the negro than in *Uncle Tom*. For instance, in one scene here a benevolent white lady experiments with the virtues of her slaves, who develop under her kind treatment a most unusual forbearance and self-control. Upon one occasion she calls them together, and taking up the matter of the disappearance of some cake from the store-closet, says:

". . .Now, you know. . .that I have no objection to your having some. If any of you would enjoy a piece of cake, I shall be happy to give it to you; but it is not agreeable to have things in my closet fingered over. I shall therefore set a plate of cake out every day, and everybody that wishes to take some I hope will take that." Well, my dear, my plate of cake stood there and dried. You won't believe me, but in fact it was not touched.

The incident of the neglected cake is, of course, used to point a moral, found in the comment which follows, " It isn't such a luxury to white children to be thought well of, to have a character."

At times, too, the negroes in *Dred* use surprising English. They indulge in remarks like "Ah! do hear the poor lamb now! 'nough to break one's heart " and " then speak your brother fair." When Dred himself is not quoting the Bible outright, his language is modelled closely upon it; and as for dialect, that he scorns utterly.

Once more, however, Mrs. Stowe partly redeems her sorry work by occasional realistic episodes. One who has witnessed a negro camp meeting will recognize some elements of truth in her account of Tomtit's "experiences." Better still is the characterization of old Tiff, who despite the author's exaggeration appears fundamentally lifelike, for one thing speaking usually as a slave might be expected to speak. Typical is his reply when asked whether he can read:

"...Why, no, honey, I donno as I can rightly say dat I'se larn'd to read, caus I'se 'mazing slow at dat ar; but den I'se larn'd all the *best words*—like Christ, and Lord, and God, and dem ar—and when dey's pretty thick I makes out quite comfortable."

Typical too is his discourse to one of his white protégés on " nigger talk ":

" ' Member you mustn't talk like old Tiff, 'cause young ladies and gen'lmen mustn't talk like niggers. Now I says dis and dat, dis yer and dat ar; dat ar is nigger talk."

But usually he succeeds best in short speeches like "de debil...got dat ar man 'fore now."

Tiff is by far Mrs. Stowe's most realistic negro, in speech, in action, in outlook. The trusted and responsible slave of an aristocratic family, in some ways he suggests both the idealized Page negro of the eighties and the very earthly Uncle Remus. No situation shows him to better advantage than when, much concerned over properly bringing up the children of his departed mistress, he holds forth on his religious duty towards them:

" You see, Miss Nina, what I'se studdin' on lately is, how to get dese yer chil'en to Canaan; and I hars fus with one ear, and den with t'oder, but 'pears like I an't clar 'bout it, yet. Dere's a heap about most everything else, and it's all very good; but 'pears like I an't clar all about dat ar. Dey says, 'Come to Christ;' and I says, ' Whar is he, any how?' Bress you, I *want* to come! Dey talks 'bout going in de gate, and knocking at de do', and 'bout marching on de road, and 'bout fighting and being soldiers of de cross; and de Lord knows, now I'd be glad to get de chil'en through any gate; and I could take 'em on my back and travel all day, if dere was any road: and if dere was a do', bless me, if dey wouldn't hear old Tiff a rapping! I 'spects de Lord would have fur to open it—would so. But arter all, when de preaching is done, dere don't 'pear to be nothing to it. Dere an't no gate, dere an't no do', nor no way; and dere an't no fighting, 'cept when Ben Dakin and Jim Stokes get jawing about der dogs; and everybody comes back eating dere dinner quite comf'table, and 'pears like dere wan't no such thing dey's been preaching 'bout. Dat ar trouble me—does so—'cause I wants fur to get dese chil'en in de kingdom, some way or other."

Tiff's comments are not only amusing but frequently sensible, suggesting a man primitive, whimsical, in some ways heroic, but withal alive and breathing. For once, in her desire to show the loving faithfulness of the slave, Mrs. Stowe chanced upon a characterization which even inconsistencies could not reduce to a puppet.

Dred himself, however, is more a problem than Uncle Tom. A weird creature, in whom are mingled traits of the African conjuror, the slave revolutionist, and the Hebrew prophet, he was evidently intended for an African Amos. Mrs. Stowe thought of him as coming upon a wicked, slaveholding world with some of the force, boldness, and picturesqueness of the Hebrew critic of society. If, then, he suggests the African only in the instinct which impels him to retreat to the wilds of an impenetrable swamp, and in those mysterious incantations which proclaim his kinship with the Congo sorcerer, we should remember that he was not intended to appear representative of the great mass of his people, but as an outstanding exception.

It is easy to conjecture how the character of Dred evolved in the author's brain. She had at hand stories of two remarkable negro insurrectionists, Nat Turner and Denmark Vesey, and also the description of a giant African whose very appearance suggested heroic leadership.[8] Furthermore, since she was devoutly religious and knew her Bible well, it was an easy step to conceiving an individual with the ability and looks of these notable negroes and the spirit of the ancient prophet. The resulting character was of course artificial, but in many respects the most interesting of all her creations.

Dred personifies merely the sterner side of the negro, the soul of the race in protest against slavery; he is a warning to whites that holding a people in bondage may not always be safe—that all captives are not Uncle Toms and old Tiffs. Uncle Tom had made the sentimental appeal of the Christian murdered by a brutal master; Dred made the more austere appeal of the intelligent bondsman aroused to righteous anger. Needless to say, the former proved more potent, so that *Dred* never remotely rivalled *Uncle Tom's Cabin* in popularity.

---

[8] In 1855 Mrs. Stowe read in manuscript and wrote an introduction for Parsons's *Inside View of Slavery,* in which she found the description of a giant slave named Dread, who seems to have been the original, at least in physical appearance, of her character. See *Inside View,* 224 ff.

With all her faults, Mrs. Stowe commends herself to us in some ways. The undeveloped state of the novel and the regrettable literary tastes of the fifties were partly responsible for her artistic defects. As a reformer she was less partisan and bitter than most of her co-workers. It is to her credit that she tried to be fair in her accounts of slavery—to show the softer aspects as well as the evils. Even though Uncle Tom and Dred are not true to life, the fault was not with Mrs. Stowe's honesty, for, faithful to her imagination, she presented the negro as she knew him, or thought she knew him.

Whatever we may say of his imperfections, Uncle Tom himself has at least rubbed elbows with the immortals of fiction, has for many years now made much stir in the world. It is doubtful whether the character is strong enough in itself to remain in the company of the elect, yet Uncle Tom may live on because of historical interest—because once upon a time, fictional character though he was, he helped settle the destiny of a great nation.

C. *The Supporters of Mrs. Stowe*

Possibly the full-fledged antislavery novel would have appeared before the Civil War even if there had been no *Uncle Tom's Cabin.* Unlike the fiction written by defenders of slavery, the antislavery novel did not spring up overnight, as it were, but developed gradually through several decades. Besides the slave narratives and earlier attempts at fiction already considered, there yet remain for mention several significant early attempts at treating the slavery problem in didactic narratives. In 1839 was published *The Kidnapped Clergyman,* a crude play in which a too comfortable and complacent minister of the Gospel is converted to Abolitionism by means of a dream, in which he is captured as a slave, his wife and daughter sold from him, and the whole family informed that as some one else's property they have no right to such peculiarly Causcasian possessions as thoughts and feelings. More significant still was Mrs. Sophia L. Little's *Thrice through the Furnace* (written about 1850), for though puerile in conception and execution, the book showed how the Abolitionists were turning to the novel as an implement in the fight.[9] "A year before the appearance of *Uncle Tom's*

---

[9] The book was published in 1852, after the appearance of *Uncle Tom's Cabin,* but the author maintained that she had written it two years previously—a statement supported by internal evidence.

Cabin, Mrs. Emily C. Pierson brought out *Jamie Parker the Fugitive* (Hartford,1851), a characteristic antislavery presentation of
a Virginia plantation that emphasized the darker aspects, such as
the heartlessness of the master, the cruelty of the overseer, the
separation by sale of members of the slave family."[10]

All this does not detract from the significance of Mrs. Stowe.
She it was who precipitated the direct contest between the two opposing sorts of slavery fiction. The struggle did not develop in-
stantly, however, for although *Uncle Tom* provoked the South to
prompt rejoinder, the Northerners considered Mrs. Stowe's remarkably successful book too powerful, too great, to be rashly imitated
by another. It ran through one mighty edition after another, and
only after the torrent of replies seemed partly to be carrying the day
by sheer vehemence did other antislavery novels appear. Once they
had taken up the work, however, Mrs. Stowe's fellow-novelists
hailed her as their leader, praising her great masterpiece, defending
it against the attacks of Southerners, themselves repeating her
themes and characters. The number of little Evas, George Harrises,
Elizas, *et al.,* swelled into a veritable tribe.

Abolitionist fiction ranged from Mrs. Phebe A. Hanaford's
negligible *Lucretia, the Quakeress* (1853) to the highly successful
Neighbor Jackwood (1857) of J. T. Trowbridge.[11] In 1855, which
was the great harvest year of this fiction, appeared Adams's *Our
World,* the most elaborate of the antislavery novels; *The Planter's
Victim,*[12] a book of the direst villainies; and Mrs. Pike's *Ida May,*
an ably written but unconvincing account of a Northern white girl
kidnapped and carried into slavery. The next year, 1856, saw the
publication of two outstanding books: Mrs. Stowe's *Dred* and
"J. B." 's *Wolfesden,* in which a planter, whose mother turns out
to have been partly negro, is himself almost enslaved. In 1857
appeared Trowbridge's *Neighbor Jackwood,* a book affording animated pictures of New England society, but almost spoiled by a
disgusting admixture of Abolitionist sentimentality. The marriage

---

10 Quoted from Gaines's *Southern Plantation,* 40-1. The present writer has
been unable to examine Mrs. Pierson's book.

11 Other trivial volumes, written chiefly for children, are: *The Young
Abolitionist* (1848), *Gertrude Lee, the Northern Cousin* (1856), *The Child's
Anti-Slavery Book* (1859).

12 In 1860 the title of this melodramatic story was changed to *The Yankee
Slave Driver,* when it was republished without change—and also without indication that it had ever appeared before.

of its white hero to the partially African heroine, however, did not bar *Neighbor Jackwood* from public favor, for like *Uncle Tom's Cabin* it had a successful career both as a novel and as a play. Another work of the same year, Denslow's *Owned and Disowned*, is overdrawn in the extreme: in addition to being sold by her own father, the heroine endures enough lesser woes to wreck several lives. The motif of the persecuted white heroine was brought to a full flowering in 1859, when Boucicault produced his sensational play, *The Octoroon*, which, next to Mrs. Stowe's masterpiece, made the greatest impression on the age, and which, melodramatic though it is, is still a work of art. Boucicault was more literary artist than reformer, as was also Mrs. Metta V. Victor, whose excellent romance, *Maum Guinea and Her Plantation Children*, was published in 1861. One of the last books of the class, *Peculiar*, appeared as late as 1863. Named after its hero, the novel suggests in title alone the convictions of the author—the negro's full name is Peculiar Institution.

Antislavery fiction is so intensely partisan largely because the authors were small-minded, but in part, also, because the Southern defenders had forced them to extremes. In attacking the slaveholders, Abolitionist romancers took little pains to be accurate, least of all about the African character, which was ruthlessly butchered and laid upon the altar of propaganda. Although by the late fifties the negro had appeared so frequently in American fiction that certain of his mannerisms and traits were well known, Mrs. Stowe's followers reflected them but superficially; mostly they assigned to him the capabilities, mannerisms, and traits which would best fall in with the assumptions of their humanitarian doctrines.

Especially did these authors delight in persecuted heroines. They turned instinctively from devout Uncle Toms to suffering Elizas, recognizing in the wronged slave woman a still stronger sentimental appeal, especially when she was relentlessly pursued by some white rake. Outstanding among these luckless ones were Brown's Clotel, Trowbridge's Charlotte, Victor's Maum Guinea, and Boucicault's Zoe.

Not content with this appeal to the chivalry of the reader, Abolitionists tried, by making many of their characters almost white, to work on racial feeling as well. This was a curious piece of inconsistency on their part, an indirect admission that a white man in chains was more pitiful to behold than the African similarly placed. Their most impassioned plea was in behalf of a person little resembling their swarthy protégés, the quadroon or octoroon. Brown's Clotel, for example, is said to have been the almost white daughter of Thomas Jefferson, and worse yet, Ida May is no negress at all, but a little white girl carried by kidnappers into bondage. Able authors like Boucicault and Trowbridge realized fully the power of the theme—realized that of all the aspects of slavery this was the most touching not only as propaganda but also in its possibilities in the drama and fiction.

Here, however, our concern is with the genuine black, who is usually a minor character, and who provides the few scraps of realism this fiction contains. A good example is found in *Clotel* (1853), a romance by the unpolished and ignorant negro writer, William Wells Brown. This fugitive slave, who tried hard to outdo all the Garrisonian cohorts in damning the South, paused occasionally in his tragedy-laden pages to introduce scraps of genuine negro dialogue and characters that he knew at first hand. Thus, apparently without realizing it, he admitted material which ill supported his boastful claims for the enslaved race. No one can doubt that the author knew personally the original of Sam in *Clotel;* still Sam is a bad argument for racial equality:

...Sam, being a " single gentleman," was unsually attentive to the " ladies " on this occasion. He seldom or never let the day pass without spending at least an hour in combing and brushing his " hair." Sam had an idea that fresh butter was better for his hair than any other kind of grease ; and therefore, on churning days, half a pound of butter had always to be taken out before it was salted. When he wished to appear to great advantage, he would grease his face, to make it " shiny." On the evening of the party therefore, when all the servants were at the table, Sam cut a big figure. There he sat with his wool well combed and buttered, his face nicely greased, and his ruffles extending five or six inches from his breast. . . .Although Sam was one of the blackest men living, he nevertheless contended that his mother was a mulatto, and no one was more prejudiced against the blacks than he. A good deal of work, and the free use of fresh butter, had no doubt done wonders for his " hare " in causing it to grow long, and to this he would always appeal when he wished to convince others that he was part of an Anglo-Saxon.

Exaggerated though the account is, it contrasts favorably with most other scenes in *Clotel*—scenes in which the author strained to insert pathos and horror, to become the relentless tragedian.

Few of Brown's co-workers, however, succeeded in constructing even brief scenes as reminiscent as this of actual life among slaves, for being usually Northern men, they seldom knew their subject intimately. An exception was Colburn Adams, whose gloomy and one-sided *Our World* is interspersed with scenes and dialogues reflecting intimate knowledge of the negro. The intelligent preacher, Harry, exhibits, at least superficially, the deeper and more promising qualities of the negro—his ambition to learn, to think, to be free. Commendably drawn, too, is Daddy Bob, the incarnation of faithfulness, who eludes the slave dealers, joins his master in prison, helps and supports him, finally comforting him in death, only to be shot as a vagabond "nigger" by inhuman slave-hunters, who seek the reward for exterminating a pest. Bob's qualities nearly all run true to form, but withal he is not well-rounded; nor are any of Adams's characters.

More consistently able was Mrs. Victor, who handled her situations well and drew lifelike people. Although uneven and upholding the doctrine of the intermarriage of the races, her work was not designed to serve a didactic purpose; rather it was a purely literary treatment of Abolitionist material, of situations and characters of immense contemporary interest. Nevertheless, *Maum Guinea* is closely akin to antislavery fiction, differing mainly in that its calmer tone allows a more convincing blending of the good and evil pictures of Southern life.

The author's introduction to the volume contains such sane and pertinent comment that one wonders how it could have been penned in the turbulent year 1861:

> Negro life, as developed on the American Plantations, has many remarkable as well as novel features. The native character of the black race under the slave system is toned down rather than changed. We find among the slaves all those idiosyncrasies which distinguish the negro type in its native land. Superstitious, excitable, imaginative, given to exaggeration, easily frightened, improvident and dependent, he forms a most singular study; and, so differently do the negro character and the relation of slave and master impress different observers, that the philanthropic world is greatly at a loss for some settled opinion regarding the normal condition of the African in the drama of civilization.

In writing of the race, I have sought to depict it to the life. Seizing upon the Christmas holidays as the moment when his exuberant, elastic nature has its fullest play, I have been enabled, in the guise of a romance, to reproduce the slave, in all his varied relations, with historical truthfulness. His joys and sorrows; his loves and hates; his night-thoughts and daydreams; his habits, tastes and individual peculiarities, I have drawn with a free, but I feel that it is a perfectly just, hand. . . .

"Maum Guinea" has not been written to subserve any special social or political purpose. Finding, in the subject, material of a very novel and original nature, I have simply used what was presented to produce a pleasing book.

Although this undertaking to depict the African type "to the life" was ambitious and cannot be pronounced entirely successful, still no other book in its class approaches *Maum Guinea* as a study of the subject.

In summary, then: aside from a few effective scenes, antislavery fiction went far afield in handling the negro character. In style and literary qualities the work of some of the Northerners was passable, but they lacked the advantage of knowing the negro and plantation life at first hand. If the Southerners erred in making the slave more childish, more rascally, more the contented buffoon than he really was, the Abolitionists erred in differentiating too little between him and the white man and in pointing out, as typical, the slave whose ancestry was largely European. At best their characterizations were slightly better than worthless.

D. *Proslavery Fiction*

When in 1852 Mrs. Stowe attempted to show the world a true picture of slavery, most Southerners felt that she had struck at their honor. Indignation and anger soon gave way to an acceptance of her challenge, and they met her with her own weapon—the novel. Up to this time Southern writings on slavery had been confined largely to political dissertations, sermons, and argumentative discourses. Fictional treatments were hardly thought of. If we except *Swallow Barn, The Recollections of a Southern Matron, Virginia Illustrated,* and other such books offering in their attractive pictures an indirect defense, there remain but few strictly proslavery narratives of an early date—only such tenth rate works as *A Sojourn in the City of Amalgamation* (1835), a disgusting satire directed against miscegenation, *Judith Bensaddi* (1839),[13] a story in which the Abolitionist heroine sees the error of her opinions, Thompson's *Major Jones's Sketches of Travel* (1848), which contain argumentative sections, and a few others. Until 1852 the South complacently trusted in tract and oration as sufficiently convincing in defending her peculiar institution, but with the advent of *Uncle Tom's Cabin* matters were altered. The charges against the slaveholders must be repelled as forcibly as delivered, and with some of their reputed hot-headedness the Southerners responded.

Yet it was not the ablest writers among them who sprang to the defense. The best of them refused to become scribbling propagandists. Simms and Cooke continued their wonted ways, turning out uncontroversial romances till the hour of the war, and even after; Poe was dead, and had he been alive, would most surely have kept out of the squabble; the new generation, including Harris, Pyrnelle, and Bonner, was hardly out of the cradle. The proslavery fiction which soon began to deluge the country was mostly the work of men and women hitherto unknown, little recognized by serious critics at the time, and now wholly forgotten.

The first wave came hard upon the appearance of *Uncle Tom's Cabin* and lasted two or three years. Then there was a lull in the production, followed by a second wave in 1859 and 1860. Before hostilities interrupted, more than thirty novels had appeared.[14]

The Southerners made it perfectly clear whom they were answering. Mrs. Stowe was named in preface after preface as well as in the stories proper. Many another Uncle Tom came scampering on the scene, but this was a very different character from the martyred hero of the Abolitionists—either a happy soul who had no foolish desire for freedom, or else a lazy scoundrel who ought to be in chains, who, in fact, would be a burden to himself and the world if anywhere else. There were even counterparts to little Eva, but these were smiling black urchins, happier and more fortunate in bondage than Mrs. Stowe's misplaced angel had been in freedom.

The South was not content with answering merely Mrs. Stowe

---

13 Published in *The Southern Literary Messenger.*

14 The list of proslavery novels is too long for this place. The best of them are discussed in Jeannette Tandy's "Pro-Slavery Propaganda in American Fiction of the Fifties," *South Atlantic Quarterly,* 21: 41-50 and 21: 170-8.

and the North, but also turned vehemently on the British, who had not only welcomed *Uncle Tom* enthusiastically, but had for years been making war on the South's "necessary" institution.[15]   To both enemies the South retorted that British and Northern white laborers were treated far worse than the slaves on the cotton plantations, and that the pictures of these slaves as brutalized and unhappy were deliberate fabrications.

In making such retort, of course, the Southern champions produced exceedingly unfair and vindictive tales.   They set forth the Abolitionists as out-and-out wretches, the Southern slaves as happy and prosperous.   They declared the South a land of law and justice, where above all places in the world men considered the rights and happiness of others.   The planter, they maintained, was a benevolent patriarch, watching with tenderest care over his family and a group of slaves too childish to take care of themselves, and fortunate to have such merciful protection.

As contrasted with the fiction of the opposing party, proslavery fiction usually deals with the genuine black, not the sentimental, abused quadroon; and in it, too, the negro is, on the whole, more realistically presented.   This superior performance was owing, not to any unusual honesty among Southern writers—for they were nowise behind their opponents in assigning to the African the thoughts, feelings, and abilities that best supported their cause— but rather to having the slaves themselves always in sight, so that, whether or no, they could scarcely go so far astray.   Neverthless, their analysis was too superficial, too much warped by prejudice, to produce more than a few lifelike and fairly consistent pictures of the negro.

The number of negro characters, good and bad, is so great that even were they better portrayed, we should not have space here to discuss them all.   A few of the most typical and significant must represent their fellows.

In one of the earliest novels, W. L. G. Smith's *Life at the South, or "Uncle Tom's Cabin" as It Is* (1852), the slaves are a lazy, shiftless lot, who give the just and kindly overseer many anxious mo-

---

15 See especially Chase's *English Serfdom and American Slavery* (1854), Southwood's *Tit for Tat, a Reply to Dred* (1856), Thompson's *Slaveholder Abroad* (1860), and Grayson's romance in verse, *The Hireling and the Slave* (2nd ed.—1855).

ments.[16] Especially is he troubled by one old man, the once exem-
plary but now rebellious Uncle Tom, who without apparent reason
(except that an Abolitionist had instilled into his head some foolish
notions about freedom) turns against his master. Finally he decides to leave his happy cabin for an unknown and misty free country somewhere north. Captured in his first flight, he is promptly
released by his master, who tells him to run northward to his heart's
content, that already there are too many trifling negroes on the plantation to support. This announcement greatly rejoices Tom, who,
failing to persuade good old Aunt Dinah, his wife, to accompany
him, sets out, day-dreaming of a happy region ahead—a kind of
Ethiopian heaven, where he will be honored and loved. But no
such land can he discover. Worn-out, starved, insulted, tricked,
he finally meets his master on a journey to the North, and asks
mercy. After many entreaties and a good deal of intercession by
the planter's family, the long-suffering owner, out of pure unselfish-
ness, allows Tom to return. Whereupon we are given to understand
that Tom was doubtless ever after satisfied with his easy chains,
and cured of his strange and unnatural longing for freedom. Of
course this is no study of a living person; Uncle Tom simply acts
out a little proslavery theory, which proves to be a farce. He is
so inaccurately presented that today he fails even as a burlesque.

One burlesque of the period, however, we cannot ignore. Mrs.
Flanders's *Ebony Idol* (1860) gives as fantastic a treatment of the
negro character as was ever perpetrated. This time a quiet little
New England town is suddenly turned upside down by the Abolitionist craze. The Curean African Aid Society finds a fugitive to
adopt—one Caesar, a fugitive as undeserving but nevertheless as
striking as ever broke chains. At first he is hailed as a hero, and
for a time continues as such, but presently his habits of sleeping
on the minister's dining room table and frightening little Lucy almost into fits impel the man of God to get rid of him. He refuses
to work, he accepts all kindnesses as his due, and finally he arouses
the ire of Miss Dickey, the town heiress, by soundly kicking her
dog, Sir Mortimer, and brutally killing her pet cat, Euphemia, after
the creature had scratched his face. Eventually he becomes such
a pest that the town shuffles him off in disgust.

---

16 Some of the scenes in this book are taken verbatim from Simms's romances, the wood-cuts are from *Swallow Barn,* and at least one of the characters is borrowed from Mrs. Gilman's *Southern Matron.*

Of course Caesar is a caricature. His highly overdrawn and misrepresented characteristics are designed to illustrate the depravity or degradation of his race—to show the unfitness of slaves for freedom. Caesar is inconsistent, at times appearing highly intelligent, at others unbelievably stupid. His actions are not motivated. He steals too outrageously and is altogether too ungrateful and insolent. Even when probable, his actions are so overdrawn as to appear foolish, so that a charitable estimate would be to call the character an embodied satire, a ridiculous burlesque—as little credit to a race as Swift's Yahoos.

A more calm and serious attempt at characterization is found in John W. Page's *Uncle Robin* (1853). Here the hero is happy, humble, contented, but yet able to think for himself. He thinks, of course, in the right direction, for slave that he is, he can still see that the African occupies the only position possible for him in America. That he can think at all, however—that he rather than a master realizes how fortunate he is—is some concession from a proslavery novelist, a tacit admission of some human ability:

> " Masser, I tells you de plain truth when I says yes [that I should rather be slave than free]. Dis, sir, is no country for free black man; Africa de only place for he, sir. I 'vise de young ones, sir, whose masters want um to go to Africa, to go dar; but I too old, sir, to go to Africa."

Robin is also pious, and exercises his intellect on religious matters. This is not surprising, for in most polemical novels of the kind, slaves are encouraged to be religious.

By all odds the best study of the negro among proslavery novels is found in Mrs. Eastman's *Aunt Phillis's Cabin* (1852), one of the most earnest answers to Mrs. Stowe. Less extravagant than her co-workers, the author undertook a sane and realistic interpretation of the negro—that is, sane and accurate in comparison with the works of others, although she was indeed partisan enough. The African she held to be incapable of taking care of himself, but happy and contented in servitude; to free him would be impracticable—a harm to both races. She drew unfair pictures of the Abolitionists, showed the Southern planter in an exceedingly favorable light, and answered Mrs. Stowe directly. Nevertheless, her book is not to be passed over lightly.

Knowing the negro well—that she did, one cannot doubt—Mrs. Eastman failed to do full artistic justice to her knowledge, especially in the matter of his idiom. At one time Bacchus says, " I shall, indeed," and at the next, " Lor, Miss Janet, I ain't so mighty ole now; be sure I ain't no chicken nuther." If dialect is to be used at all, there should be more consistency, more doing away with the r's, the use of more conjunctions. On the other hand, she noticed that negroes like big words, that they glory in show and finery, and that their humor is spontaneous and natural. There is a sparkle in Uncle Bacchus's account to his wife of seeing a ghost:

> " Your head was mighty foolish," said Phillis, " and you just thought you saw it."
> " No such thing. I saw de red eyes—Aunt Peggy's red eyes."
> " High!" said Phillis. "Aunt Peggy hadn't red eyes."
> " Not when she was 'live!" said Bacchus. " But thar's no knowin' what kind of eyes sperrits gets, 'specially when they gets where it ain't very comfortable."

This Bacchus is the author's masterpiece, a far more convincing character than Aunt Phillis, his wife, who, largely white, is thrifty, ambitious, and rather given to thought, and whose constant aim is, moreover, to crush out the African crudities of her troublesome spouse. To this program Bacchus refuses to subscribe—a happening which should delight us, for whitewashed he would be less interesting, less the delightful old rascal he is. So well characterized is Bacchus that it is easy to predict his actions under most circumstances. He will always seize the smallest excuse for getting drunk; he is naturally happy-go-lucky and carefree; he is most dignified just after receiving a new lot of his master's cast-off clothes; when dressed gaudily he can pray or speak in church with the greatest unction; he is master at making excuses and begging favors; he is musical to a fault and plays the banjo as only a negro can; he thinks his master the greatest man in the world and apes him in everything; he likes to talk of George Washington, whom he says he still remembers; and he hates Northerners and poor whites. He longs for a ruffled shirt, but when Phillis makes him one, thinks it proper to appear none too well pleased, because she has done no more than her duty and praise might spoil her; he even complains of the garment and brings on the unlooked-for result of having it shorn of its ruffles, whereupon he thinks himself mightily abused. In many ways a " gentleman of color," he is an arrogant boaster and swaggerer, envied and respected by all his less fortunate fellows.

Well conceived though he is, Bacchus suffers from the author's carelessness and omissions, and at best adequately represents but one side of the African nature. If a few of Aunt Phillis's commendable qualities could have been blended with his more boisterous ones, the result might have been one wholly satisfactory characterization. Even so, Bacchus is the most successful figure in proslavery fiction.

Yet neither Bacchus nor Uncle Tom nor any of their tribe is an entirely satisfactory creature of fiction; they are all burlesqued or artificial or incomplete—either too much the buffoon or the savage or the gloomy-minded, refined captive, all reflecting the literary weakness of their day or the partisan sentiment of the slavery struggle. The complete oblivion which has engulfed them is a sure index of the extent to which they were walking arguments; of them all only Uncle Tom survives, and he lingers on mainly because of a glorious past record. Of course they are not alone in their inefficiency, for likewise gone are the conventional African puppets of our pre-War literary artists. The leisurely sketches of *Swallow Barn* may still be read, but not for any negro character in them. Poe's *Gold-Bug* and Simms's romances will not continue in vogue because of their Jupiters or their Hectors, but if at all for widely different reasons.

All of them, whether the creatures of the literary artist or the reformer, had their day; and all of them, taken together, served a quite recognizable service. Through them, as pioneers of the type, was slowly built up an understanding of African traits and mannerisms, an understanding among both authors and readers. The dialect writers of the eighties owed more to their predecessors— men who discovered the literary possibilities of the negro without fully using them—than either they or the world has supposed.

There never was, and is never likely again to be, such intense interest in the negro as in the decade preceding the Civil War. He was championed by the Northerners, depreciated by the Southerners, and lionized by the British. For a few brief years he was the main actor on the stage of the Western world; and those who wrote his most telling lines—for the moment, at least—were the slavery romancers.

CHAPTER VII

RUSSELL, PAGE, AND THE BEGINNINGS OF THE NEW ERA

After the Civil War American literature acquired fresh vigor. The upheaval of military struggle helped set in motion new literary forces—a seeking after realism, a feeling that the present held more than the past, an interest in native American subjects. " The eight years in America from 1860 to 1868," says Mark Twain, " uprooted institutions that were centuries old, changed the politics of a people, transformed the social life of half the country, and wrought so profoundly upon the entire national character that the influence cannot be measured short of two or three generations."[1] The whole country was affected by the far-reaching activities of the war, and men and women exposed to gruesome sights and even more gruesome stories of blood and pillage were in no mood to enjoy sentimental stanzas on the rainbow or tame stories of domestic bliss. Now the great mass of readers wanted more lifelike heroes and heroines, more meaningful experiences, more distinctive types; and their demands were supplied in the fiction which grew up in the following decade—fiction primarily on American subjects. "America, shaken from narrow sectionalism and contemplation of Europe, woke up and discovered America. In a kind of astonishment she wandered from section to section of her own land, discovering everywhere people and manners and languages that were as strange to her even as foreign lands. . . . In twenty years every isolated neighborhood in America had had its chronicler and photographer."[2]

The new day was heralded by the appearance of a new kind of literature from the West—the Pike County ballads. Bret Harte and John Hay were the pioneers in producing these short poems, which depended for their effectiveness on the accuracy with which they reflected the traits of a locality. Provincial types, peculiar dialects, strange modes of life were seized upon as likely materials, and were presented in both prose and verse to an interested public. The Creole of Louisiana, the mountaineer of North Carolina and

---

[1] Quoted from Pattee's *History of American Literature since 1870*, 6.
[2] Ibid., 15.

Tennessee, the Hoosier of Indiana, and the negro of the cotton states all came forth as companions to the Pike of Harte and his fellows.

More than any other section, the South offered the sort of literary material which was now demanded. Writers were quick to see this, and in the eighties they exploited the region so thoroughly that Professor Pattee well calls the period " The Era of Southern Themes and Writers." Discussing this era he writes: " Nowhere else were to be found such a variety of picturesque types of humanity: negroes, crackers, creoles, mountaineers, moonshiners, and all those incongruous elements that had resulted from the great social upheaval of 1861-65. Behind it in an increasingly romantic perspective lay the old regime destroyed by the war; nearer was the war itself, most heroic of struggles; and still nearer was the tragedy of reconstruction with its carpet-bagger, its freed slaves, and its Ku-Klux terror. Never before in America, even in California, had there been such richness of literary material."[3]

Especially did able Southern men of letters turn their attention to the negro, of whom they made the most popular of all local American types. Not that the new age discovered, or rediscovered, him, but rather that it saw in him now, clearly and with delight, possibilities which before had been but lightly esteemed. As a tragic figure he was still neglected, but his irresistible gaiety, his gift for dance and song, his spontaneity and childish delight in gay colors and all forms of display, his love of high-sounding words, his fondness for chicken and watermelon, his gullibility, his excuse-making powers, his whimsicality, his illogicalness and superstition, his droll philosophy, his genial shiftlessness and laziness, " his superb capacity for laughter "—these traits were appreciated as never before, were revalued and pronounced delightful. His very speech was thought worthy of study, so that story-writers painstakingly mastered the intricacies of his idiom. All of this is not to say that from the seventies and eighties on the negro wholly escaped the superficial portrayal of earlier times, but rather that a number of able authors, for the most part Southerners, created negro characters which are more successful and lifelike than any before seen.

---

[3] Pattee, 295-6.

I

The fresher, more penetrating treatment of the negro did not appear unannounced. There was a clearly marked transition from the old—a time when the old superficial school and the newly arisen realists continued side by side. Books of the pre-War variety lingered on, and not only survived the transition, but continued even after Russell, Page, and Harris had entered upon the scene. Hungerford's *Old Plantation* and Simms's romances were reissued. Echoes of the War were still heard in Kirke's *On the Border* (1867) and Locke's *Swingin' Round the Cirkle* (1867), two of a large class of publications whose authors seemed unable to forget earlier successes with war audiences. Lingering Abolitionist sentiment cropped out in Louisa May Alcott's *Work* (1873), in which the hero marries the heroine despite her African taint. Slave narratives appeared occasionally until the end of the century. Paul du Chaillu's *Stories of the Gorilla Country* (1867) continued a fashion for writing about the parent land of the slave. Bagby's *Old Virginia Gentleman* (1884), Smedes's *A Southern Planter* (1887), and numerous other memoirs and reminiscences of *ante-bellum* Southern society were well received. John Esten Cooke pursued his way undisturbed by the War, except that now his heroes were generally officers on the Southern side in the recent struggle; toward the negro he retained his old attitude. Even Sidney Lanier's *Tiger Lilies* (1867), fresh and striking as is some of its material, considers the African as the conventional menial, to be taken as part of the setting and sketched superficially. It was not until eight years later, in his dialect poems, that Lanier really awoke to the possibilities in the realistically drawn negro.

Another product of the transitional period was a revival of the old controversy between North and South, this time not over the slave, but over the new freedman. A second group of Northern partisans began to denounce the iniquities of the South in re-enslaving the negro by disfranchising him. Foremost among them was Albion W. Tourgee, a Northern Federal judge who, coming to North Carolina and hastily looking around him, came by the mistaken notion that he understood the emancipated black well enough to interpret him to the world. His novels are little more than well written political tracts. Nor are the more readable ones of Constance Fenimore Woolson, who was more the artist than reformer, of any enduring value as pictures of the South or of the negro; she understood Southern conditions and people but superficially.

As the century advanced, both this political fiction and the belated echoes of the recent struggle grew more infrequent, and after 1880 they counted for little. Both types were pushed aside by the new movement that depended on a far kindlier interest of the sections in each other.

II

In the awakened enthusiasm for Southern themes and types which began about 1875, we cannot overestimate the importance of the old *Scribner's Monthly*. This magazine specialized in up-to-date contributions, and opened wide its pages to new literary ventures, especially those dealing with provincial life. In 1873-4 *Scribner's* published Edward King's articles on " The Great South," which contained realistic illustrations and descriptions of largely unknown nooks and corners, whose very existence was unsuspected by Northern readers. In addition to introducing the region, the magazine brought before its readers some of the South's most famous men of letters. *Scribner's* discovered Cable, was largely responsible for the widespread vogue of Russell, introduced Page and Gordon to the public, and increased the prestige of Harris. The magazine attempted to keep up with the times, and among its experiments was a comic section called " Etchings," consisting mainly of skits and anecdotes. When this section presently became popular, it was enlarged and the name changed to " Bric-a-Brac." Here were published Irish comical anecdotes, short articles in various dialects, little amusing compositions in verse, and finally poems in negro dialect. Sometimes, too, there were comic etchings. The influence of all these upon several young Southern poets, presently to be considered, is highly important. More significant still, as early as July, 1871, *Scribner's* carried in its regular pages a negro dialect poem, "Caesar Rowan," which although in no other way noteworthy at least showed the trend of literary taste.

Before 1875 Sherwood Bonner was contributing negro dialect stories to a Northern paper, and at about the same time Mollie E. Moore Davis was publishing in *Wide Awake* "Snaky Baked a Hoe-Cake," "Grief," and similar tales. Mark Twain's *Old Times on the Mississippi* (*Atlantic,* 1875) and *Tom Sawyer* (1876) reflected convincingly the author's early acquaintance with the slave; his *Gilded Age* (1874), written in collaboration with Charles Dudley Warner, contained a situation well suited to the approaching era of realism, an old blind negro's listening in consternation to the noise of the first steamboat on the Mississippi River—a situation which the Lanier brothers utilized a few years later in a dialect poem. If there were any point in doing so, a long list of other publications might be cited here, illustrating the gathering interest in the negro.

III

The new post-War interest in the negro did not, however, originate in fiction, or in prose at all, but in balladry—balladry written by a group of young Southern poets: the Lanier brothers, Paul Hamilton Hayne, and Irwin Russell, among whom the unfortunate Russell was outstanding as pioneer. Sidney Lanier appears to have been the first actually to turn to negro balladry,[4] but Russell first brought the form into popularity—was the first so to use it as to attract the attention of the great reading public. Concerning his importance both Page and Harris, whose judgments were surely trustworthy, fully agreed. In an introduction to the collected poems of Russell, Harris wrote: " Irwin Russell was among the first— if not the very first—of Southern writers to appreciate the literary possibilities of the negro character, and of the unique relations existing between the two races before the war, and was among the first to develop them." Page's words are still more significant: " It was the light of his genius shining through his dialect poems—first of dialect poems and still first—that led my feet in the direction I have since tried to follow." Not only Page and Harris but a throng of others were incited to imitate Russell's method in his contributions to *Scribner's*. Just as he himself was undoubtedly influenced by predecessors, so practically all who have worked the same vein since his day have owed something to him.

As a youth Russell was in the habit of annoying the family cook by burlesquing, extemporaneously, the doleful tunes she sang as she went about her work. Later on, when he had outgrown such practices, he amused himself with the comic section in *Scrib-*

---

[4] See " The Power of Prayer," by Sidney and Clifford Lanier, *Scribner's Monthly*, June, 1875.

ner's. When the Pike County ballads began to appear, he read them avidly, fascinated by the type. Presently he tried his hand at writing some skits in dialect, several of which were published in the local paper. Finding it so easy to burst into print, he sent other pieces to *Scribner's.* " Uncle Cap Interviewed " was accepted for the number of January, 1876, and its success at once launched him upon a fitful and brief career as a literary man.

Few authors have so well understood the negro, and except for Harris, few have portrayed him so faithfully and penetratingly. Upon this aspect of his work, rather than upon poetical technique, Russell's fame will ultimately rest. Although incidentally his dialect verse is genuinely poetical, it is mainly valuable as a study of character—as setting forth a type of humanity at once delightfully primitive, whimsical, humorous, and serious. At times, no doubt, Russell treated his subject with exaggerated levity, but on the whole his work shows complete sympathy and understanding, and a desire to present the African fairly.

Most of his verse was written for the section in *Scribner's* called " Bric-a-Brac "—a department given over almost wholly to humor. For instance, when Russell's favorite " Nebuchadnezzar " appeared, it was illustrated with cuts showing the unfortunate plow-boy soaring high in air, followed closely by his uprooted plow, with the treacherous little beast below in a kicking posture impossible to even the most vindictive mule. Writing for such a comic section meant, of course, subordinating poetic art to entertainment, but it did not necessarily destroy the essential truth of the presentation. In actual life the negro is prince of comic characters, and to show this comedy in him is not inevitably to exclude all else. Beneath the sparkling humor—often the sheer ridiculousness—of Russell's lines, there is usually something deeper for the reader prepared to understand it. Russell was fascinated by his subject, and wrote not only with enthusiasm but with complete sympathy.

His dialect ballads are more realistic than romantic. Even the idealized "Christmas Night in the Quarters " contains enough realism—in the dialect, in the convincing actions of the characters, in their attitude toward the world, particularly toward the whites—to throw the balance, to make the scenes first of all true to the world of fact. In his frequent references to the past, the poet makes little attempt to defend the slaveholding regime by dwelling on its glory,

its romantic appeal; rather he simply utilizes as literary material
the wreck of plantation society; he refers to past days mainly because he finds them attractive. If his negroes remember the period
before the War, they never, for a moment, forget the present. In
" Mahsr John," for example, the former slave ponders with regret
on the past greatness of his old master, when

> " Ol' Mahsr John wuz pow'ful rich—[and] owned a heap
>   o' lan':
> Fibe cotton places, 'sides a sugar place in Loozyan';"

and when

> ". . . dere wuz forty ob de niggers, young an' ol',
> Dat staid about de big house jes to do what dey wuz tol'."

But he does not stop here; he also comments upon the present regrettable condition of that once splendid planter:

> " Well, times is changed. De war it come an' sot de niggers
>   free,
> An' now ol' Mahsr John ain't hardly wuf as much as me;
> He had to pay his debts, an' so his lan' is mos'ly gone—
> An' I declar' I's sorry for my pore ol' Mahsr John."

Many of those who came after Russell overlooked the present in
sighing over a social order forever gone from the earth. Russell
himself rarely got far away from what he could actually see around
him—from contemporary types, from the ordinary sights on the
plantations and in the country stores.

With certain knowledge he touched upon practically all the
negro's characteristics—in " Uncle Nick on Fishing," his superstition; in " Norvern People," his confused, ignorant, but definite
opinions of the outside world; in " Wherefore He Prays That a
Warrant May Issue," his feeling, developed through years of dependence in slavery, that he has a natural right to steal from and be
supported by the whites; in " Uncle Cap Interviewed," his loqua-
city; in " Pot-Liquor " and " Nebuchadnezzar," his habit of talking
to animals as though they understood him; and in most of the poems
his religiousness, his childlike attitude toward nature, and his inimitable humor. The negro's interpretation of the whole universe
and of all the past in terms of his own day is well illustrated in
numerous passages, as when Booker, the banjo-player, sings of how
Noah kept abreast of the times:

" Dar's gwine to be a' oberflow," said Noah, lookin' solemn—
Fur Noah tuk the " Herald," and he read de ribber column—
An' so he sot his hands to wuk a-cl'arin' timber-patches,
And 'lowed he's gwine to build a boat to beat the steamah
     Natchez.[5]

The negro's sermons, too, are distinguished by their contemporary interpretation of the Bible. His use of specific terms, especially of homely figures, is frequently reflected:

You all know de story—how de snake come snoopin' 'roun',—
A stump-tail rusty moccasin, a-crawlin' on de groun',—
How Eve an' Adam ate de fruit an' went an' hid deir face,
Till de angel oberseer, he come an' drove 'em off de place.[6]

The qualities of the rising young generation of negroes, and the inevitable differences and even conflict between them and their old-fashioned parents, developed into one of Russell's favorite themes. " Dat Peter " and " Precepts at Parting " show the subject at its best.

Of all his works Russell himself liked most the short, highly comic skit, " Nebuchadnezzar," which despite its cleverness, its sheer comedy, cannot be ranked as his strongest work. The piece depends too much upon situation and is too brief to be rated with several of the poet's longer studies of the negro. Undoubtedly his masterpiece is "Christmas Night in the Quarters," a tiny, idealized epic of *ante-bellum* plantation life, with clear-cut, lifelike pictures and an animated reflection of the holiday spirit in the cabins. This one poem alone would insure the author an enduring position among Southerners.

In discussing Russell's work, Joel Chandler Harris called his dialect " not always the best—it is often carelessly written." Before taking this statement too seriously, however, one should remember that the critic was himself the ablest writer of that dialect who has yet appeared. Measured by the standards of before the War, Russell's lingo is a distinct advance, and indeed it has seldom been surpassed since. He clung to the homely, quaint, vivid negro idiom; he spelled sanely and with reasonable consistency; and above all, he reproduced the sparkle and spontaneity so typical of the negro's speech. That in his hasty writing he was at times a little careless—as when he wrote, " It's hard on your mudder, *your* leabin' "—is the worst charge which can be brought against him.

---

[5] *Christmas Night in the Quarters*, 18.
[6] Ibid., 76.

Russell created no distinctive negro characters; his work was rather commentary on a race, generalization on a type. He showed the likableness of the negro people, their appeal as literary subjects, and especially how dialect could be used effectively in their portrayal. To the last he wrote in the same vein, and at the time of his death was even planning a novel with negroes as principals in the story. His restless and impatient genius, however, was unsuited to novel-writing; moreover his later poems, though slightly more subtle than his earlier ones, showed little promise of anything greater to come, so that, after all, perhaps he had contributed the best that was in him. The four years preceding his death, in 1879, were rich in accomplishment, and like his literary heirs we can only be glad he had done so much.

IV

Shortly after 1876 other Southern authors stepped forward to join in the work, and to rival what Russell had already done. The latter's plan to write of the negro in prose was sound, for henceforth it was to be in prose that he was best portrayed. Verse offered so many limitations to subtlety and sustained characterization that most who, like Page and Gordon, began by imitating Russell's ballads eventually turned to the short story or the novel.

As already noted, before 1875 Sherwood Bonner had published dialect stories in a Northern newspaper; in 1880-1 she began contributing to *Harper's Monthly;* in 1878 appeared her *Dialect Tales,* and in 1884 her *Suwanee River Tales.* Although Miss Bonner's characterization was superficial and her dialect far inferior to that of Russell, she found ready acceptance for her work. By 1880 dialect stories were so much in demand that magazine editor and publisher alike welcomed them, and even began a search for new writers. Joel Chandler Harris, for example, had no sooner proved in the columns of his newspaper his ability in the field than *Scribner's* solicited his stories, and a publisher suggested that he get out a book.[7]

The greatest find of the magazine, however, although not the ablest portrayer of the negro, was George W. Cable, discovered in 1873 by Edward King for *Scribner's.* Between 1873 and 1877 he published in that magazine several powerful stories which at-

---

[7] This he did in 1880—*Uncle Remus: His Songs and His Sayings,* published by D. Appleton & Co.

tracted little attention as they first appeared, but which when collected in the volume, *Old Creole Days* (1879), became the sensation of the day. The negro enters in only two or three of these stories—principally in " 'Tite Poulette " and " Posson Jone," where he is not the chief actor. Perhaps, however, the enthusiastic reception of Irwin Russell and the vogue he established had something to do with Cable's writing, in 1881, " Madame Delphine," supreme in American literature as the tragedy of a woman damned by a slight African taint. Such a subject Cable handled gloriously; he did not, however, concern himself actively with the genuine black, nor perhaps could he have been a master here. Again, Cable's peculiar powers showed to advantage in *The Grandissimes* (1880), where he dwelt with sustained intensity upon the ever-present, lurking, mysterious danger to the whites in holding slaves—in keeping in subjection a race but recently savages and still retaining much of their African weirdness and superstition. "His characterization of the voodoo quadroon woman Palmyre with her high Latin, Jaloff-African ancestry, her ' barbaric and magnetic beauty that startled the beholder like the unexpected drawing out of a jeweled sword,' her physical perfection—lithe of body as a tigress and as cruel, witching and alluring, yet a thing of horror, ' a creature that one would want to find chained '—it fingers at one's heart and makes one fear."[8] Even this unusual side of the African Cable treated mainly because it blended well with the romantic material furnished by the picturesque and varicolored decay of the old Creole civilization of New Orleans. The ordinary negro, the comic, earthy, realistic character of the workaday world, held very slight attraction for the romancer; Cable's genius demanded more far-removed and mysterious personalities, and with them he usually worked.

V

The magazines also offered the first encouragement to another young man destined to succeed in literature, Thomas Nelson Page. Here again Russell's poems proved a beacon light, for they guided Page into the field of literature which he afterward made particularly his own. Page, in fact, was the founder of a school of glorifiers of the *ante-bellum* South, writers who, in their indiscriminate

---

[8] Pattee, 250.

love of everything belonging to the old South, grew as enthusiastically fond of the negro as had the Abolitionist earlier. Theirs was,
of course, a different kind of regard—a sentimentality which made
for a more convincing picture of the negro, because growing out of
first hand knowledge, but which, for all that, was still sentimentality.

In 1877, a year after Russell's advent, Page published in *Scribner's* his first dialect poem, "Uncle Gabe's White Folks," which
contains the germ of all he was to write later in his romances of
Virginia. In the same year Page's friend, A. C. Gordon, also contributed to *Scribner's* a dialect poem, similar in spirit and manner.
Presently the two began writing together, publishing jointly, in
1888, a volume of verse, *Befo' de War,* which they dedicated to
Russell. For many years after, they wrote on the negro, but with
this collaboration of 1888 they parted amicably, and in the years
that followed Page left his less gifted friend behind.

By birth and training Page was an aristocrat, and as one he
wrote. The scion of an old Virginia family, living at a time when
the generation of gentlemen-planters to which his kindred belonged
was giving way before the new tribe of business men and commer-
cial folk, and the society which they had erected not only vanishing
from the actual world, but, as he feared, from the memories of men,
he felt it a duty to interpret a glorious past to an uncomprehending
world. Much of what he wrote is an artistic defense of the old
regime. The defense is, to be sure, excellent literature, but in
writing it Page was not so much the literary artist as the faithful
clansman, the historian, as he would have it, of Virginia's "first
families." It was partly in a spirit of defense that he wrote those
notable stories finally published in book form as *In Ole Virginia*
(1887)—an American classic. Page never again reached the high
level of this work; as the years passed he repeated himself with increasing ineffectiveness, and although most of his later books are
fairly commendable, never again did one come so near to showing
genius. His most polemical work is the novel *Red Rock* (1898),
" a chronicle of reconstruction," which is so evidently partisan that
it fails completely as art. To friends of Page it is comforting to
think that the author's reputation will not depend wholly on such a
book; there will always be left " Marse Chan," " Unc' Edinburg's
Drownin'," and " Meh Lady."

Page is most successful with the negro when he considers him as a part and parcel of the past. The freedman he drew no better than did a hundred others. His negro cut off from an all-absorbing past or from association with aristocratic whites—or even when shown living during the era before the War, instead of looking back on it in sad retrospect—is one-sided and usually overdrawn. Uncle Jabe of " Uncle Jabe's Marital Experiences " might do for the comic stage or the joke book, but that is all. Old Hanover of " P'Laski's Tournament " and George Washington of "George Washington's Last Duel " may serve to amuse us, but both are unreal. Page was unsuccessful, too, in portraying the negro woman; none of the striking black mammies of fiction are from his pen. In " Mam' Lyddy's Recognition " the reader hopes at first to find a nurse true to life; instead he encounters a crudely disguised puppet, an artificial creature designed to show the undesirability of the newly spoiled negro who demands " recognition " without so much as knowing the meaning of the term. Treating such a subject was not Page's forte; he was at his best only when describing life in a patriarchal and feudal South. When the slave can live over again in memory the humble but at the same time important role of the past, when he is the spokesman through whom we learn of those past days of glory, then he is likable—then he is Page's triumph.

Even at best, however, he is scarcely individualized. Page created no great characters. but rather reproduced types—especially one notable type, best represented by Sam of " Marse Chan " and Billy of " Meh Lady." These paragons of the race are what Page thinks the negro ought to be, their attitude the attitude he ought to take, their dependence his normal status. In their way, these old negroes are gentlemen, and they know their place in respect to the whites:

> Instantly, and as if by instinct, the darky stepped forward and took the bridle. I demurred a little; but with a bow that would have honored old Sir Roger, he shortened the reins, and taking my horse from me, led him along.[9]

By nature they are servants, but they have more than a servant's interest in the " family " and in their responsibility. They take an untiring interest in even the love affairs of their masters:

> " Well, I got one o' de gent'mens to write Judy a letter for me, an' I tole her all 'bout de fight, and how Marse Chan knock

---

[9] *In Ole Virginia*, 4.

Mr. Roony over fur speakin' discontemtuous o' Cun'l Chahm-
b'lin, an' I tole her how Marse Chan wuz a-dyin' fur love o'
Miss Anne. An Judy she gits Miss Anne to read de letter fur
her. Den Miss Anne she tell her pa, an'—you mind, Judy
tell me all dis arfterwards, an' she say when Cun'l Chahmb'lin
hear 'bout it. . . .

" We didn't know nuthin' 'bout dis den. We wuz a-fightin'
an' a-fightin' all dat time; an' come one day a letter to Marse
Chan, an' I see 'im start to read it in his tent, an' his face hit
look so cu'ious, an' he han's trembled so. . . . An' what yo'
'spose 'twuz?

"He tuk me wid 'im dat evenin', an' tell me he had done
got a letter from Miss Anne."[10]

These old friends and followers are too good to be true, and they
are, after all, imaginary creatures. They do not belong to the real
world in which lives Uncle Remus, who eats, and makes horse-
collars, and talks more about himself than about the people of Miss
Sally's household. They are highly idealized—glorified creatures
of a doting romancer. They fit perfectly into the strangely convincing but unreal stories that they tell. " Surely no freed slave
ever told a consecutive tale like that, perfect in its proportions and
faultless in its lights and shadows, yet such a criticism never for a
moment occurs to a reader. The illusion is complete. The old
South lives again and we are in it both in sympathy and comprehension."[11]

Not that with all this illusion Page fundamentally misrepresented the negro. Perhaps realism is no more necessary for success here than in other characterizations. Since the African is so
patently a fun-loving, earthy, happy-go-lucky type, the realist has
usually succeeded best with him, yet who can deny that Page, too,
has succeeded with his glorified old black aristocrats? If his success is not that of the thoroughgoing psychologist or the newspaper
reporter, it is nevertheless success.

Page's nearest approach to realism is in the use of dialect, which
he employs with undeniable power. The sound of the negro's voice,
his homely idiom, his cast of sentence, his peculiar exclamations—
all these are faithfully reproduced. Old Sam's words,

" He's Marse Chan's dawg, an' he's so ole he kyahn git long no
perter. He know I'se jes' prodjickin' wid 'im,"

---

10 Ibid., 30-2.
11 Pattee, 267.

might well have been taken down verbatim from some actual speaker. Even in the midst of the narrative proper he sometimes interrupts with realistic exclamations:

"Hows'ever, dey sut'n'y wuz sot on each urr an' (*yo heah me*) ole marster an Cun'l Chahmb'lin dey 'peared to like it 'bout well ez de chil'en."

But these realistic interjections are, after all, few. The dialect, too, is smoothed out by the powerful sweep of idealization. The sentences are too orderly, the transitions too effective, the words too much to the point. Like the old speakers themselves, at bottom the speech is true to life, but it, also, is too nearly perfect to be an accurate reflection of nature.

We can say fairly of Page, then, that in his romancer's way he portrayed well a certain aspect of the American negro, a side best exemplified in the household slave of the aristocratic Virginia planters. His devotion to a beloved master, his pride in the " family," his scorn of both blacks and whites who are not of the best quality, his courteous manners—all this Page clearly emphasized; but further the romancer's attitude would not allow him to penetrate. It would not allow him the subtlety necessary to lay bare the more complex nature of the real negro. Page did not consider the negro a sufficient interest in himself, and failed to set him forth subjectively except in the one mood of regretting emancipation and the passing of " the good old days." He could not consider him separate from the past and from a white master class. Page has achieved enduring fame as the loyal defender of Virginia plantation life before the War, as the romantic interpreter of a society in which there was much that is beautiful and noble, even as the genial painter of the African in a certain mood; he will not, however, pass into history as a great creator of distinctive and lifelike negro characters.

VI

By 1885 negro dialect writing was a fashion of the hour and Page only one of a number engaged in producing it. His contemporaries were numerous and frequently able, but from the group one man stands out as the master—Joel Chandler Harris.

Chapter VIII

UNCLE REMUS ARRIVES

If justice be done him, Joel Chandler Harris will be known to the future as the supreme interpreter of the American negro in his most attractive period of development. In the transitional period just after the Civil War, when the old negro of slavery times had not been quite supplanted by the free-born generation which we know today; in a day when the old negro was suspicious of the new, and the new was scornful of the old; in an age when the old loyalty and the new independence were still existing side by side; when the group of rural phenomena which had once formed the whole of the negro's surroundings, and had supplied all the material for the play of his fancy, was rapidly being enlarged to include all the man-made contrivances of the city—it was in this time that Harris lived and wrote. The negro of his writings, who belonged to the eighties and nineties of last century, has passed from the stage, and into his place has stepped the free American black—a quite different person. For literature, the change is regrettable. Looking dispassionately at the two, one cannot help feeling that the older is the more attractive. Just as Cooper caught the Indian at the fortunate moment when he was close enough to white civilization to be somewhat understood, and yet far enough away, with his bloody tomahawk and hellish warwhoop, to be safely interesting, so did Harris catch the negro in his most picturesque state, when, retaining the quaint beliefs, superstitions, folk-tales of past benighted years, and his old primitive outlook on life, he emerged into the fierce light of a freedom which confused and troubled him and thus made him all the more appealing. Harris was truer to life and abler in his presentation than Cooper, for Cooper read much of his own racial feelings and philosophy into the Indian hero. Most of the great creators of characters in our language—Shakespeare, Chaucer, Thackeray—have interpreted their own race, have worked with characters whose ways of thinking have been largely the same as the author's. But Harris has gone outside himself, and has entered into the thoughts and feelings of a human type different from his own in spirit, in psychology and emotional temper, in disposition, in talents and preferences; and has laid bare the very soul that he found there.[1]

Neither in his own charming little autobiographical fiction, *On the Plantation* (1892), nor in the able biography by Julia Collier Harris, is there much said about Harris's early years in the Georgia town of Eatonton, where he was born and spent the first thirteen years of his life. These years were important because during that time he was brought into close contact with the humble race which befriended him and which he has made known and liked wherever English is read. An illegitimate child, he was probably conscious of this misfortune when with people of his own race; at any rate, he frequently sought companionship among the black servants of the town and neighboring plantations, who were themselves lowly and unfortunate and who would naturally care nothing for his illegitimacy. Doubtless no other writer has ever come so close to them in spirit, has ever shared so much of their sympathy, has ever seen them so much at their best, has ever entered so thoroughly into their minds and souls. His interest was continued throughout a lifetime.

When about fourteen years old, the youth went to work on the plantation paper of Mr. Joseph Addison Turner, gentleman, planter, literary critic, and journalist, living about nine miles from Eatonton; and here young Harris was thrown more than ever into contact with the slaves he already liked and understood so well. One of his first deeds, so he tells us, was to succor the runaway slave Mink, thus winning the respect and devotion of all Mink's hundred and more friends. "When the work and the play of the day were ended and the glow of the light-wood knot could be seen in the negro cabins, Joel and the Turner children would steal away from the house and visit their friends in the slave quarters. Old Harbert and Uncle George Terrell [the original of Uncle Remus] were Joel's favorite companions, and from a nook in their chimney corners he listened to the legends handed down from their African

---

[1] After reading Harris's letters, one cannot, to be sure, escape the conclusion that he projected some of his own personality into the character of Uncle Remus. A second reading, however, will convince anyone that he carried over only the characteristics he had in common with the negro—his sly wit, his geniality and good humor, and a turn of expression which the slave doubtless helped to form. These are only a few of Uncle Remus's traits; there are others, African at bottom, which could have been known only to one who thoroughly understood the negro soul.

ancestors—the lore of animals and birds so dear to every plantation negro. And sometimes whilst the yellow yam baked in the
ashes, or the hoe cake browned in the shovel, the negroes would
croon a camp-meeting hymn or a corn-shucking melody. The boy
unconsciously absorbed their fables and their ballads, and the soft
elisions of their dialect and the picturesque images of their speech
left an indelible imprint upon the plastic tablets of his memory."[2]
For several years he shared the confidence of the whole quarters,
and came to know its life with a thoroughness never surpassed and
perhaps never equalled.

Nor was it only through accident of birth and through being
thrown so intimately into contact with the Turner negroes that
Harris became the most able presenter of their psychology. By
temperament he was suited to put himself into the place of his
dusky friends, and share their feelings, their enthusiasms, their
joys—their attitude toward a puzzling world. With a sympathy
and understanding of others, and a modesty and self-effacement
which made it easy to go out of himself and understand another
mind, he united the flashing wit, the keen perception, the genial
humor of a healthy intellect, and an astonishingly long and accurate
memory. He remembered not only what he had seen and heard,
but the accompanying words and actions, down to the smallest item.
Both through environment and mental equipment, he was suited to
give the world an accurate portrayal of the negro.

Harris, of course, was not conscious during these early years
that he was studying a human type or that he was training himself
for a literary career. Doubtless it was best so. Because he learned
his subject leisurely, naturally, without conscious effort or system,
his treatment was all the more sure, all the more artless and spontaneous. Later he listened to new stories and to new story-tellers
to obtain fresh material, but he listened also because he was interested in the speakers. He never set about studying his subject
scientifically; he had already studied unconsciously in boyhood, in
those days when his constant friends were the lowly Africans who
cheered him and welcomed him, and of a night told him stories
about Brer Rabbit and Brer Fox.

---

[2] Julia Collier Harris: *Life and Letters of Joel Chandler Harris,* 33-4.

Too much has been made of Harris's contributions to folk-lore.[3] In his *History of Southern Literature,* for example, Carl Holliday speaks of " his unique contribution to folk-lore " and contends that because they are folk-literature " these tales will live on and on. For folk-literature has ever been the most permanent part of the world's literature." In the first place, the truth of the assumption is doubtful, but more serious is the neglect of the literary excellence of Harris's work. These same critics who harp so much on the value of the Uncle Remus tales as folk-literature usually fall into another error, which unfortunately is held by some who avoid the first—that Harris was first and last and only a journalist. He was, of course, a professional journalist, but he was a great deal more besides. That he gave his best years to writing for his paper is undeniable, and both in private conversation and in print he insisted that he was only an unpretentious newspaper man who had made one or two literary ventures and was on no account to be considered a man of letters. Yet he developed into one of the South's most able writers. A critic usually so careful as Professor Pattee goes wrong on this matter:

> . . . Never once did he seek for publication; never once did he send a manuscript to any publisher or magazine that had not earnestly begged for it; never once did he write a line with merely literary interest.[4]

Harris did write without being solicited by publishers: a little reading of his biography and letters shows how much thought and time he gave his books as the years passed. Far from being an uninspired and perfunctory journalist, as some would have us believe, Harris was at heart a poet. Here and there in his pages one runs across passages of surprising beauty which flash out all the more forcibly because they are embedded in prose marked by simplicity and directness. His style suited perfectly his material, and so well did he blend excellent material with simple dignity, directness of expression, and sincerity of feeling that his best books have become classics. Despite his modest contentions, then, he was much more than a mere recorder of folk-stories.

The stories are themselves by no means to be despised. They

---

[3] Harris's Uncle Remus was not the first plantation story-teller. Earlier specimens of the type are found in *Anti-Fanaticism* (1855), *Home and the World* (1857), *Maum Guinea's Children* (1861), and other novels.

[4] Pattee, 303.

comprise most of the oral tradition and literature of the quarters, and are written in such realistic form that they might well have been taken down verbatim—as indeed some of them were. Yet, valuable though they are, their setting and the characters who tell them are worth far more. Mark Twain was right when he wrote once to Harris:

> " You can argue *yourself* into the delusion that the principle of life is in the stories themselves and not in their setting, but you will save labor by stopping with that solitary convert, for he is the only intelligent one you will bag. In reality the stories are only alligator pears—one eats them merely for the sake of the dressing."[5]

Or to put it another way, we tolerate the stories to get what comes with them—the scene in the humble cabin, the incidental remarks of the speaker, the characterization of the story-teller himself. All Harris required was the bare outline of the folk-tale; he gave it its dressing, putting it in words he knew the speaker would use— words which he had heard used over and over again.

In depicting the negro Harris was, in his best work, a consistent realist. Allied in spirit to Russell, he looked at the old South as it actually was, or at most cast only a moderate amount of glamor over its story. He was the antithesis of Page not only in making the negro the chief interest in himself, but in looking with calm eyes at an attractive state of society which was yet not all sweetness and light. Uncle Remus's " Marse John," for example, was only a private in the Northern army who, rather ignominiously shot out of a tree by the old man himself, as he was preparing to kill a Southerner, marries Miss Sally, the young lady who nurses him back to life. Page would have made the Northerner an officer, a gallant young cavalier, who rescues the Southern heroine at the most spectacular moment in the most spectacular manner, and as a spectacular climax, marries her after a romantic courtship. Upon such an occasion Page's negroes would have commented upon the perfection of the two—at least of the heroine. Uncle Remus, however, sees the foibles of his white friends as well as their virtues; and unlike Page's creatures, he thinks more often of himself than of " the family." Of Miss Sally, daughter of his mistress of slavery days, he says:

> " 'T ain't so much what she say. . . . ez de way she do. I

---

[5] *Life of Harris*, 69-70.

bin knowin' Miss Sally ev'y sence she wuz a suckin' baby, and
I ain't never is see her show de white er her eye like she done
des now."[6]

Remus's every word and action suggest the actual; we are cast under
no illusion in reading of them, but feel that they belong to life.
Note, for instance, how convincing is the scene in which Uncle
Remus meets the train bearing the Northern visitor, whom he has
never seen:

> "Ain't dis yer Miss Doshy?"
>
> Turning, Miss Theodosia saw at her side a tall, gray-haired
> negro. Elaborating the incident afterward to her friends, she
> was pleased to say that the appearance of the old man was
> somewhat picturesque. He stood towering above her, his hat
> in one hand, a carriage-whip in the other, and an expectant
> smile lighting up his rugged face. She remembered a name
> her brother had often used in his letters, and, with a woman's
> tact, she held out her hand, and said:
>
> " Is this Uncle Remus?"
>
> "Law, Miss Doshy! how you know de ole nigger? I
> know'd you by de favor; but how you know me?" And then,
> without waiting for a reply: " Miss Sally, she sick in bed, en
> Marse John, he bleedzd ter go in de country, en dey tuck'n
> sont me. I know'd you de minnit I laid eyes on you. Time
> I seed you, I say ter myse'f, ' I lay dar's Miss Doshy,' en, sho
> nuff, dar you wuz. You ain't gun up yo' checks, is you? Kaze
> I'll git de trunk sont up by de 'spress waggin."[7]

Uncle Remus's stories told to Miss Sally's " little boy " are ever
mixed with remarks about the world around him. He comments
upon the horse-collar he is making, or upon what is to be served
for dinner, or upon the general " cussedness " of " sunshine niggers,"
or upon a thousand and one things which would be interesting to
a genuine Remus of some actual place in Georgia.

In all these remarks his dialect is the best to be found anywhere;
it is convincing to the very smallest phrase. It was largely, or
mainly, because of his mastery of the vernacular that Harris
achieved his triumph. " I have Mr. Harris's own word for it,"
wrote Walter H. Page in 1881, "that he can *think* in the negro
dialect. He could translate even Emerson, perhaps Bronson Alcott,

---

6 *Uncle Remus and His Friends*, 257.
7 *Uncle Remus: His Songs and His Sayings*, 202-3.

in it, as well as he can tell the adventures of Brer Rabbit."[8] Moreover, he enjoyed his work. " . . I am very fond of writing this dialect," he once admitted. " It has a fluency all its own; it gives a new coloring to statement, and allows of a swift shading in narration that can be reached in literary English only in the most painful and roundabout way."[9] In reporting realistic negro dialogue Harris has never been surpassed.[10] He reproduced a thousand homely phrases to be found nowhere else in print. Other writers have given individual words, phrases, and speeches as genuine as his; but in successfully continuing the dialect through page after page, even through volume after volume, without becoming artificial or involved and without lapsing into mere provincial English, he stands alone. So uniformly excellent is his work that any page of it will show the greatness of his mastery.

Harris treated the negro not as a type, but created distinct personalities. In this he rose superior to Russell; and in making them characters of a real contemporary period rather than of an *antebellum* age of romance, he towered above Page. Billy of " Meh Lady " and Sam of " Marse Chan " established a type, which subsequently has been repeated by Page and successfully copied by Hopkinson Smith, A. C. Gordon, James Lane Allen, and others. But Harris's characters are far more individual; it is quite unlikely that any one can ever produce a fresh Daddy Jake or Free Joe or Minervy Ann or Mingo; and it is well night impossible that there will ever arise another Uncle Remus. He is as distinct a personality as the Wife of Bath or Bottom the Weaver or Colonel Newcome, and yet he is more than an individual. Despite an obvious individuality, he typifies the whole negro race as it was in that momentary and evanescent phase following emancipation.

Of all his characters, Harris's favorite was Free Joe, as pathetic a figure as one would wish to find in literature. The narrative of which he is the hero has never been fully appreciated, for although it is a notable American short story, few people have read it. In simple but impassioned language Harris tells of the tragedy of an extremely harmless but persecuted black man, the veriest of fortune's fools. Cut off from his own race by the stroke of manumis-

---

[8] *Life of Harris,* 164.
[9] Ibid., 403-4.
[10] Harris heard the Gullah dialect but little, and hence reported it weakly; C. C. Jones surpassed him here.

sion, deprived of white protection in a slaveholding world, forbidden by his humble condition to leave the state, held to the unsympathetic community where remained all that was dear to his simple soul, he was forced to realize that " though he was free he was more helpless than any slave. Having no owner, every man was his master. He knew that he was the object of suspicion, and therefore all his slender resources (ah! how pitifully slender they were!) were devoted to winning, not kindness and appreciation, but toleration; all his efforts were in the direction of mitigating the circumstances that tended to make his condition so much worse than that of the negroes around him,—negroes who had friends because they had masters."[11] Misfortune came upon him at every turn. He was not allowed to visit his slave wife; a spiteful master finally sold that wife away to keep him from meeting her in the woods; his little dog Dan was killed; and despite their own miserable condition, even the poor whites who tolerated him because of the petty services he rendered them would not, or could not, sympathize with him. They insisted that since he was a " nigger " he could not suffer; he was of necessity happy. And so Joe smiled outwardly and suffered inwardly—alone, misunderstood, without a sympathetic human tie of any kind. It was the tragedy of a well-meaning soul hopelessly out of place in the world and with no friends. At last he was found one day in the woods dead, his hat off, his head bent, " as if he had bowed and smiled when death stood before him, humble to the last."

Another character of which Harris was very fond was Aunt Minervy Ann, a negro mammy as well drawn as any in fiction. Not only is she the faithful guardian of the Perdue family, but she is an aristocrat of her race, the descendant of an African prince, "Affikin fum 'way back yander 'fo' de flood, an' fum de word go." In every way she is a " character," and like all Harris's figures was modelled upon an actual person—this time upon one of Harris's cooks.

Then, again, there is Mingo—once " Laughing Mingo " but now the serious old protector of his dead mistress's little girl. The contrast between him and the " cracker " grandmother, Mrs. Feratia Bivins—a woman hardened through suffering and embittered by the domination of powerful aristocratic neighbors—is all in Mingo's

---

11 *Free Joe and Other Georgian Sketches,* 8.

favor. Though Mrs. Bivins hates most " niggers " she appreciates Mingo's fidelity and moral strength.

Another important person is Daddy Jake, the old carriage-driver and friend of the children of the plantation. These children, Lucien and Lillian, miss him so much when he runs away because of the cruelty of the overseer that they set forth into the woods to find him. In their wanderings they lose their way, but most fortunately are found and rescued by their old friend. Although Daddy Jake is a paragon of faithfulness to a master, he has a mind and will of his own.

We might consider more fully here all these people—Free Joe, Minervy Ann, Mingo, Daddy Jake—but since not only the ablest but the greatest part of Harris's characterization of the negro is found in Uncle Remus, it will be more profitable to consider him to the exclusion of the others.

Uncle Remus is a former slave who has lived over into an age of freedom that perplexes him rather than advances him in life. He has seen his old mistress pass away, and all her generation ; he has watched Miss Sally, daughter of his old mistress, grow up and marry ; and he has remained in the family of his own free will, just as his forefathers had done under compulsion. Now that Miss Sally's little boy has grown large enough to take an active interest in things of this world, Uncle Remus amuses him every day with a story drawn from plantation folk-lore. Never was a story-teller— not even the immortal Scheherazade herself—so abundantly supplied with material. Never was material fresher, more free from conventionality, more pleasingly naive and original. Into the primitive land of negro folk-lore—a well-ordered little world, peopled with comfortably dressed, fun-loving, talkative beasts, strangely human in their foibles—Uncle Remus enters with the confidence of guide and interpreter, and fully informs the little boy of the various misadventures of lumbersome Brer Bear, of would-be shrewd and daring Brer Fox, of vicious Brer Wolf, and others, all of whom fall victim to the inordinately lucky and unscrupulous hero, Brer Rabbit—the most picaresque of all picaresque figures. Uncle Remus knows the personal history of all the animals—of the whole forest tribe, from mammoth Brer Elephant to inconspicuous Brer Mud " Turkle."

We are not long in discovering, what Harris and many others

pointed out, that the animals are the negroes themselves, and that Brer Rabbit represents the ideal hero of their primitive dream world—an individual able, through craft and downright trickery, to get the better of a master class seemingly unbeatable. The ideals of the animals are the negro's; their prying dispositions, their neighborliness, their company manners, their petty thefts, their amusements are all the negro's; Brer Rabbit likes the same kind of food, the same brand of fun, as his interpreter does: he has the same outlook on life. Even the hopeless incongruity of this animal world—the rabbit and the fox owning cows, and hurting their "hands," and feeling an elementary kind of responsibility for their families—is part and parcel of the negro spirit. It is a product of his primitive outlook on life, of a poetical feeling that takes no account of the hard logic of consistency.

All this Uncle Remus shows about his race without detracting from his own distinct individuality. He is always consistent, always the same genial exponent of the psychology of the negro. Although he looks with longing eyes to the past, he is not exactly sentimental about the matter; he brings the past so vividly into the present that he actually lives it over again; and moreover he never forgets the immediate moment—with its duties, its dinners, its "sunshine niggers," its talk, and its leisure. He is at once a child of the present and a torch-bearer from the past, and yet, though eminently typical of his race, he is as much an individual as Sam Weller.

More enjoyable than the stories he tells are their setting and Remus's incidental comments. Practically any of the stories will show much about the old man himself. Note, for instance, how the setting of " Brother Mud Turtle's Trickery " is employed advantageously in character portrayal:

> " I don't like deze yer tales 'bout folks, no how you kin fix um," said Uncle Remus, after an unusually long pause, during which he rubbed his left hand with the right, in order to run the rheumatism out. " No, suh, I don't like um, kaze folks can't play no tricks, ner get even wid der neighbors, widout hurtin' somebody's feelin's, er breakin' some law er nudder, er gwine 'ginst what de preacher say.
> " Look at dat man what I des been tellin' you 'bout. He let de udder man fool 'im en ketch 'im, en mo' dan dat, he let um tote 'im off to de calaboose. He oughter been tuck dar; I ain't

'sputin' dat, yit ef dat had been some er de creeters, dey'd er
sholy got loose fum dar."[12]

This passage is filled with suggestions about the speaker; it em-
phasizes his love of "getting even" with his neighbors by a kind of
trickery which, while effective, will hurt nobody's feelings, his inconsistency, his lack of sympathy for some of the white man's
established conventions, his fear of the law, and his respect for
religious tenets.   Moreover, it shows his particular idiom and a distinctive habit of speech, of repeating himself when he is pleased
with a statement or when he is firmly convinced of his opinion—
" I don't like um," repeated.   After these introductory remarks,
Uncle Remus proceeds to tell one of the stories about the " creeters "
getting loose.   It seems that once upon a time Brer Fox and Brer
Mud " Turkle " had a " fallin' out," and that Brer Fox at last gave
the enemy an advantage by fishing one day in the water near Brer
Mud " Turkle's " house:

" Bimeby Brer Fox come ter whar ole Brer Mud Turkle
live at.   I dunner what make ole Brer Mud Turkle live in such
a damp place like dat.   Look like him en his folks 'ud have a
bad col' de whole blessid time.   But dar he wuz in de water
und' de bank, layin' dar fas' asleep, dreamin' 'bout de good
times he'd have when de freshet come.   He 'uz layin' dar wid
his eyes shot, when de fus' news he know he feel sump'n nudder
fumblin' 'round his head.   'T wan't nobody but ole Brer Fox
feelin' 'roun' und' de bank fer fishes.

" Brer Mud Turkle move his head, he did, but de fumblin'
keep on, en bimeby he open his mouf en Brer Fox he fumble
en fumble, twel bimeby he got 'is han' in dar, en time he do dat,
ole Brer Mud Turkle shet down on it.   En I let you know,"
continued Uncle Remus, shaking his head slowly from side to
side as if to add emphasis to his statement, "I let you know
when ole Brer Mud Turkle shet down on yo' han', you got ter
cut off his head, en den wait twel it thunder 'fo' he turn loose.

" Well, suh, he shet down on ole Brer Fox en ef you'd 'a'
been anywhars in dat settlement you'd 'a' heard squallin' den
ef you ain't never hear none befo'.

" Brer Fox des hilt his head back en holler, 'Ouch!   Ouch!
What dis got me?   Ouch!   Turn me aloose!   Ouch!   Some-
body better run here quick!   Laws a massy!   Ouch!'

" But Brer Mud Turkle, he helt on, en he feel so much com-

---

[12] *Uncle Remus and His Friends,* 167.

fort dat he'd er in about went ter sleep ag'in ef Brer Fox hadn't er snatched en jerked so hard en a-holler'd so loud."[13]

The story continues, but this will suffice.   Here the whole range of the negro character is revealed so thoroughly that even during the narrative proper one is conscious of the pervading personality of the speaker.

Possibly, however, he appears to still greater advantage in certain sketches, not folk-tales at all, which Harris included, along with the folk-stories, in *Uncle Remus: His Songs and His Sayings* (1880) and *Uncle Remus and His Friends* (1892).   Strange to say, these sketches have been neglected by critics, yet they are not only as delightful as anything Harris ever wrote, but have no interest but Uncle Remus—not even the slight distraction of a folk-tale.   Typical is " Uncle Remus Finds a Snake," in which after the old gardener has offended his Miss Sally, she sits by the window to see that he does his work:

> . . She was not long in observing that he was in no special hurry.   He would grub away for a few minutes, and then lean on the handle of his hoe and rest.   Frequently, he would turn his hoe around, examine the blade of it, and shake his head. He seemed to get on with his work so slowly that the lady put on her sun-bonnet and went out to oversee the job.   For an hour she kept the old man busy, and he grew tired of it.   She was not in the habit of following him up so closely.   Finally, when he saw that she intended to see the yard cleaned then and there, Uncle Remus raised his head and looked all around, sniffing the air.
> " What is the matter now ?" the lady asked.
> Uncle Remus made no reply to the question, but continued sniffing the air, looking very serious.   Presently he said in a very loud and emphatic tone :—
> " I wonder wharbouts is dat snake what I bin interferin' wid ?"
> " What are you talking about ?" the lady asked contemptuously.
> " 'Bout dat ar snake what I smells.   I kin allers smell um when dey gits stirred up."
> " What snake ?" asked the lady with something more than curiosity.
> " Dat ar snake what I bin interferin' wid.   He some'rs closte 'roun' here, sho."

---

[13] Ibid., 169-70.

" Where?" asked the lady, instinctively grasping her skirts.

" Miss Sally," said Uncle Remus, in his most business-like way, "I wish you'd please, ma'm, be so good ez ter look in dat bunch er grass dar. He smells so rank he bleedz ter be right 'roun' here."

Instead of searching in the bunch of grass, " Miss Sally " jerked up her skirts, gave a little scream, and ran into the house like a deer. Safe on the back porch, she turned and looked at Uncle Remus. The old man was half bent, and his head was going from side to side. He pretended to be looking for the snake, but his Miss Sally knew that he was laughing at her. Angry as she was, she interfered with Uncle Remus no more, but left him to clean the yard in his own way and in his own time.[14]

There are many such skits, all excellent; and in each one of them appears the same quaint old man. Never for a moment does he deviate from the personality which Harris first conceived about 1880.

Uncle Remus is truly one of the great products of American literature—a lasting embodiment of what the American negro was during the period of development when he was most original and attractive, and a character which will insure Harris lasting fame. He is, to be sure, no great tragic figure, no suffering hero, torn by conflicting desires, dominated by an overwhelming passion, ruined by unworthy ambitions or mad desires, subjected to the trial of death or dire disgrace; his soul receives no such test as that afforded by a Goethe or a Shakespeare—lacking which it cannot of course measure up to the great spirit of Faust or Hamlet. But surely Harris's accomplishment is, for all that, not small. To set the negro forth in his happy, his whimsical, his pathetic mood, convincingly, true to nature, alive and breathing—to have done this is much— is, perhaps, all of which any white author, great or small, would be capable.

---

[14] Ibid., 258 ff.

CHAPTER IX

THE CONTEMPORARIES AND SUCCESSORS OF HARRIS

After Uncle Remus, the number of fictional mammies and uncles, plowboys and dusky swains, already enormous, continued to grow, until now, as one looks back in review, the spectacle appears bewildering. Negro characters are no longer to be reckoned by the hundreds, but by the thousands; the number examined for this chapter alone exceeds six hundred. In novels, plays, stories, sketches, dozens of them every year, the inevitable black servant is present, ready to usher in the guest or deliver a message or bring in the tea. The droll fun-maker, more lifelike than before Russell wrote, but still the buffoon, lingers on, none the less popular, it seems, because his remarks are old or his traits long conventionalized. Story tellers of the Uncle Remus type, although becoming less common, appear now and again; the Page butler or dignified body servant still talks of " de days befo' de Wah." And in addition, a new figure has come upon the scene: the black of the present generation, ambitious, demanding recognition, determined to fight for a place in the sun. To discuss all these systematically and thoroughly would be impracticable here; all that can be attempted is a brief survey of what has happened and is happening to the type.

From a purely artistic standpoint, it is doubtful whether any real advance in portraying the negro has been made since the publication of Harris's first books. More serious portrayals have appeared, stories more tragedy-laden, showing the hero in woeful plight; there have been more consistent attempts to keep away from the past, and to center attention on the spirituality of the man. Such recent writers as R. E. Kennedy and Mrs. Julia Peterkin throw aside much of the patronizing air of the white author, in itself a step forward; yet neither they nor others have set forth a character which is at once so convincing and appealing, which so satisfies the requirements of art, as Uncle Remus. The newer negro is, from one point of view, more striking. He is sterner, more enigmatic—a disquieting figure whose prototype from life is yet to be reckoned with as he contends " for the solid prizes of the Universe." He provokes one to think, and is withal a strong argument against racial discrimination; yet for the man of letters he has, so far, proved less attractive than the old. In becoming an over-serious type the negro has lost some of the buoyancy of spirit, the delightful naiveté, the happy spontaneity of word and act which distinguishes the characters of Russell and Harris.

Not that the latter are, as yet, in danger of being disregarded. On the contrary, they continue to flourish, and their tribe, with all its shortcomings, increases with every year. Old themes, old types, old situations are constantly reappearing.

It would be easy to illustrate how thoroughly these old types and manners of portrayal have established themselves among us. One might point to a recent volume called *Wall-Eyed Caesar's Ghost* (1925), " amusing sketches of the *old-fashioned* colored folk down South," or to *Mister Fish Kelly* (1924), which once more capitalizes the happy-go-lucky disposition of the African, or to the overdrawn stories of Hugh Wiley or Octavus Roy Cohen, which borrow copiously from both minstrel show and previous works of fiction, or to the highly popular Christmas book by Harry Stillwell Edwards, *Aeneas Africanus,* the hero of which is a Page negro undergoing strange adventures, or to A. C. Gordon's *Maje* (1914), which merely repeats successes of decades earlier.

Still another convincing illustration is found in negro balladry. Since the days of Irwin Russell this balladry has changed but little. *Christmas Night in the Quarters* aside, only one other contribution need be mentioned; Page and Gordon's *Befo' de War* (1888), which to Russell's freshness of phrase and spontaneity added a note of sentimentality, a worshipful attitude toward the past. Since 1888 many volumes of negro balladry have appeared, but none which varies much from the models set by Russell and Page.[1] Some lean more on the realism, others more on the sentimentality; only a few show skillful blending of the two. The *Bandanna Ballads* (1898) of Miss Howard Weeden is too overloaded with sad reminiscences and plaintive longings on the part of the slaves; so likewise is much of the verse of B. B. Valentine, who like Page was a Virginian and a life-long defender of the old regime. Valentine's

---

[1] Something new appeared in Mr. Vachel Lindsay's " The Congo " (1914), which so powerfully suggests the negro's imaginative power, his love of the chant, most of all his " basic savagery," explained by the centuries of cruelty and ignorance passed by his ancestors in the African jungles. This poem, however, is more ambitious in scope, and is in nowise to be classed with the balladry.

work, *Ole Marster and Other Verses,* appeared in book form in 1921, although most of his pieces were written earlier for magazines and newspapers. Others—John Trotwood Moore, for example, or Paul Laurence Dunbar—have echoed *Befo' de War,* yet on the whole Russell's work has proved the more vital model and inspiration. Such poems as Dunbar's "Accountability," "An Ante-Bellum Sermon," and "The Party" would fit well in *Christmas Night in the Quarters.* Russell's most conspicuous follower, however, was the gifted young North Carolina poet, John Charles McNeill, whose *Lyrics from Cotton Land* (1907) contains many sprightly lines, much suggestive description, many deft strokes of characterization. "The Trickster Tricked," "A Hindrance," "Selfishness," and "The Coon from the College Town" catch the negro in a happy and typical mood, and are highly successful humorous pieces. In most respects McNeill's work equals that of his master, yet one cannot help noticing that he had a master.

I

For the short story, also, models dating from the eighties have set the standard, and still continue largely to do so. Harris and Page especially, both of whom continued to write well into the twentieth century, have each had a large following.

To begin with, the popularity of the Uncle Remus stories inaugurated, it seems, a fashion for collecting negro folk-tales[2]— a fashion which spread far outside the United States, and found followers among residents of the West Indies and missionaries to the Congo. Scarcely an important African people escaped having its popular literature done into English for the amusement of our readers, while in America the Creole negroes of Louisiana and the West Indies, the "Gullah" blacks of the coast region of Carolina and Georgia, not to mention many ordinary mammies and uncles in Georgia and elsewhere, were all besieged for their legends and proverbs. Usually some attention was paid to the characterization of the speakers, as well as to the form and content of their tales, the collector being prompted as often by a literary impulse as a scholarly.

---

[2] Some collecting of negro folk-literature was done before Harris's appearance. See, for instance, William Owen's "Folk-Lore of the Southern Negroes," *Lippincott's Magazine,* December, 1877. "This article gave me my cue," said Harris (*Life of Harris,* 143). For collecting in Africa, see Callaway's *Nursery Tales, Traditions, and Histories of the Zulus,* London, 1868.

To mention only a few volumes, illustrating all classes, there appeared Louise Clarke Pyrnelle's *Diddie, Dumps, and Tot* (1882), closely modelled upon the books of Harris; Jephson's *Stories Told in an African Forest by Grown-up Children of Africa* (1893), Vaughan's *Old Hendrick's Tales* (1904), both compiled by workers in Africa; C. C. Jones's *Negro Myths from the Georgia Coast* (1888), written in the Gullah dialect;[3] Milne-Home's *Black Nurse Stories* (1890), by a West Indian collector; Owen's *Voodoo Tales* (1893); Martha Young's two books, *Plantation Bird Legends* (1902) and *Behind the Dark Pines* (1912); Alcée Fortier's *Louisiana Folk-Tales in French Dialect and English Translation* (1895), published for the American Folk-Lore Society; most important of all, Virginia Fraser Boyle's *Devil Tales* (1900), which presents with particular power various psychological aspects of the negro, especially his superstitiousness and proneness to weird imaginings. Mrs. Boyle was no mere imitator; her work shows originality and distinction, being far superior to that of most who took suggestions from the tales of Uncle Remus.

More numerous even than the followers of Harris were those of Page. As the glorification of the Old South increased, with each passing decade, Page's theme and manner grew steadily in popularity. As recently made clear in Professor F. P. Gaines's study called *The Southern Plantation* (1924), more and more were the harsher facts of slavery forgotten or ignored, increasingly did an attitude of sentimentality and kindly regard dominate the pictures of plantation society, and increasingly was the " old-fashioned darkey," along with the estate to which he belonged, the young mistress he served, the old master he aped and worshipped, fondly idealized. In such a light, more or less, was he viewed by Harry Stillwell Edwards, A. C. Gordon, John Trotwood Moore, Grace King, Ruth McEnery Stuart, Will N. Harben, Lafcadio Hearn, R. M. Johnston, Alice French, James Lane Allen, Hopkinson Smith, O. Henry, and Mrs. Burton Harrison—all in some degree upholders of the Page tradition. This group has been rivalled only by the writers of boisterous comedy—Hugh Wiley, O. R. Cohen, Irvin S. Cobb, E. K. Means, and others, who continue the custom, long established, of exploiting the incongruous and laughable in the negro. Their portrayals, however, different as they at first seem

---

[3] Cf. A. E. Gonzales: *The Black Border* (1922), stories in this dialect.

and stressing another side of the African, do not yet deny the fond themes of the Page school. The devotion of freed slaves to impoverished masters, the protection by faithful mammies and uncles of a dead master's children, an old body servant's expressed longings for past golden days, the misery coming to field hand and house servant alike when a master's family declines and his estate goes to ruin, the drabness of contemporary life among the black folk as contrasted with the ideal conditions of the past—all these and other elements derived from the plantation tradition furnished material for stories unnumbered.

These stories came from the pens of Northern authors as well as Southern. In *The Mistress of Sydenham Plantation,*[4] Sarah Orne Jewett drew a highly sympathetic picture of Old Peter, with " his scorn of modern beings and their ways," who still served his mistress, now insane through suffering, " while most of the elderly colored men and women who had formed the retinues of the old families were following their own affairs, far and wide." In *The Cloverfield's Carriage,*[5] Frank Stockton recounted how Elijah, the family coachman before freedom came, was unable to forget his once exalted position and eventually returned to resume his duties. Harriet Spofford's *A Guardian Angel*[6] presents the nurse Tolly, whose fidelity to a former mistress and her daughter is only strengthened by a legal right to leave them. And in his long story, *The Monster,*[7] Stephen Crane skilfully contrasts the childishness and vanity of Henry the groom with his staunch loyalty. Among Southern authors the number of short works of fiction glorifying plantation types has been enormous. The theme of Grace King's *Monsieur Motte*[8] is the devotion of the slave. In James Lane Allen's *Two Gentlemen of Kentucky* (1888), Peter Cotton, a fantastic old darkey, steadfastly devotes his life to Colonel Field, once his master. The perfect friendship of the two old men, and the excessive thoughtfulness, not to say heroism, of the former, are too good to be true, yet despite a conventionalized situation and impossible characters, the story somehow touches the heart. Likewise ideal is the friendship of Ben and Judas, in Maurice Thomp-

---

[4] *Atlantic Monthly,* Aug., 1888.
[5] *Century,* January, 1886.
[6] *Harper's,* May, 1897.
[7] *Harper's,* Aug., 1898.
[8] *New Princeton Review,* July, 1885.

son's story of that name;[9] but overtopping all fiction of the kind is Hopkinson Smith's novelette, *Colonel Carter of Cartersville* (1891), in which Colonel Carter, himself an embodiment of the erstwhile gentleman-planter of the South, says of his staunch friend and protector, "Chad was bawn a gentleman, and he'll never get over it." In this one statement Smith strikes the keynote of his story. Colonel Carter's instinctive courtesy, his soaring pride, his lavish hospitality in the face of bankruptcy, and an improvidence resulting from life-long residence amid luxury and plenty, mark him as belonging to the romancer's *ante-bellum* South; and by similar tokens—deference to a noble master, an unshakable loyalty, a patience and good temper which no trouble can outface, a sympathy for and an understanding of the Colonel—Chad also proves himself of the aristocracy. Neither character ever actually walked the streets of New York, or met the welcome guest at the door, but in their natural habitat, between the covers of a romancer's book, they are thoroughly convincing—and welcome company for most readers.

Occasionally, in contrast to this idealization of former slaves, appears a treatment of the negro's sordid or animal-like aspect— exemplified in Abram, the brute negro of Sarah Barnwell Elliott's *An Incident* (1899), or in Moss Harper of E. E. Peake's *Jungle Blood*.[10] These figures, however, are exceptions, for although white authors have often insisted on the negro's childishness, his condition as a natural inferior, they rarely paint him as vicious or depraved.

Perhaps there could be found no better way to gauge the accomplishment of the second generation of story writers after the Civil War than by considering the work of Ruth McEnery Stuart, a highly successful delineator of the negro, and one of the most prolific. Her success represents the best of her day, and her weaknesses are typical.

It will be seen at once that she fell below Harris at his best. Her characters are but successful copies of familiar models, her concept of the race was inherited from many literary forebears, her dialect is usually convincing and sparkling without in any way marking an advance over that of predecessors. At times Mrs. Stuart stooped to the blind glorification of the feudal past of her section, as, for instance, in *The River's Children* (1904), in which

---

[9] In the volume *Stories of the Cherokee Hills* (1898).
[10] *McClure's,* Sept., 1908.

old Hannah and Israel, steadfast beyond all belief, wait day by day in their humble abode on the levee for the return of a master whose child they protect with loving care. In addition to this sentimentality, however, Mrs. Stuart had a realistic manner; and in this lay her strength. Of the more mundane side of her subjects she made effective use, especially when, by placing them in unusual situations, she could heighten their drollery or naiveté or whimsicality. Whatever else these characters do, they seldom sit for long shucking corn or spinning yarns about Brer Rabbit or descanting on the past. George Washington Jones tries to give himself away to a white lady as a Christmas present; the widow Moriah lures Pete, an eligible bachelor, into matrimony within less than a week of well planned campaigning; Salina Sue, forced by public sentiment into a regular marriage with her common law husband, decides upon an elaborate church wedding, at which she can wear gloves and utilize the services of her fifteen-year-old daughter Lucy as bridesmaid. " Hit'll be a mighty good an' 'ligious thing for her to remember in after-years," adds the mother, in discussing the approaching nuptials. " 'Tain't every yo'ng gal dat kin ricollec' her pa an' ma gittin' married."

Mrs. Stuart's most successful characters are women—realistic women who, like Salina Sue, have strong wills and stronger voices. The slave woman Egypt " hires her time " of her master, and sets out to make money to redeem from slavery her worthless but handsome husband; through will power and impudence she succeeds. Rose Ann, washerwoman, supports her well dressed husband, but does so of her own accord and is in every way able to take care of herself. Resenting the charge that he neglects his family, she answers her husband's aspersers with vigor:

> " No, sir...my ole man he s'po'ts his family jes as much as most o' de cooks' husbands does along dis bayou, ef I ain't mistooken. I ain't tellin' no tales when I say de moes' mos' of 'em does is to tote home de heavy baskets or buckets dey wives packs for 'em in de kitchens whar dey works."[11]

Incidentally the passage offers a shrewd commentary on the negro woman, and by implication the suggestion of a racial or social problem. Mrs. Stuart frequently saw racial and social problems, but these she neglected, keeping her eye always on her characters

---

[11] *Napoleon Jackson,* 124.

as interests sufficient in themselves. She worked consistently as a literary artist; and if she added nothing new, at least she continued, with freshness and spirit, the realistic manner of Russell and Harris.

Other authors, not content with entertaining pictures of life among the lowly, have centered attention on the meaning of what was presented. Of the several problems arising out of the African's presence in America, at least one, the tragedy of mixed blood, has often attracted short story writers.

One remembers at once Mark Twain's long story, almost a novel, *Pudd'nhead Wilson* (1894), with its unforgettable account of Roxana and her white baby. Few more moving scenes exist in our fiction than that in which the slave mother informs the imperious and rascally youth, her supposed master, that he is, after all, only her son, changed in the cradle to prevent the dreaded sale down the river. The account of how he runs amuck morally, and wrecks not only his life but that of his mother and others, Mark Twain develops with power. Several strong scenes grow naturally out of the sad condition made clear in the opening pages:

> To all intents and purposes Roxy was as white as anybody, but the one-sixteenth of her which was black outvoted the other fifteen parts and made her a negro. She was a slave, and salable as such. Her child was thirty-one parts white, and he, too, was a slave, and by a fiction of law and custom a negro. He had blue eyes and flaxen curls like his white comrade, but even the father of the white child was able to tell the children apart—little as he had commerce with them—by their clothes; for the white babe wore ruffled soft muslin and a coral necklace, while the other wore merely a coarse tow-linen shirt which barely reached to its knees, and no jewelry.[12]

More poignantly tragic, though not so well rounded or permanently convincing, is Kate Chopin's *Désirée's Baby*.[13] In this a young Louisiana planter falls in love with and marries the fair Désirée, a girl of unknown parentage. To them is born a child, which soon proves by unmistakable signs to be part negro. The supposition follows naturally that Désirée is of slave descent; and heartbroken, cast off by her unfeeling husband, she kills herself. The deed has hardly been discovered when the husband, by an

---

[12] *Pudd'nhead Wilson,* Uniform ed., 23.
[13] In *Bayou Folk* (1894).

unlucky accident, learns that he it was who had the taint. Here the story ends—suddenly, dramatically, overpoweringly tragic with its intensity and latent suggestion of heartaches and terrors. Few situations in our literature so grip the heart or shock by their awfulness.

Other problems—whether, for example, whites are ever justified in mistreating the negro who displeases them, as in Norman Duncan's *Hypothetical Case,*[14] or the predicament of the white boy who loves a negro girl, as in Margaret Deland's *Black Drop*[15]—have furnished themes for stories; but on the whole the novel or play, rather than the story, has been favored by those attracted primarily by sociological perplexities. The short story has rarely been written from any but a purely literary purpose; and whatever explanation may be offered, the brief narrative form, settled upon by Harris and Page, and adopted by many followers, has accorded most of the satisfactory presentations of the negro character so far made.

II

In the novels and plays since 1870, negro characters have rarely appeared as heroes—that is, until recent years. They have, however, continued to be important minor characters, and seldom has an author drawn sweeping pictures of American life, at least Southern life, without including the colored maid, the droll gardener, or the pompous and dictatorial black cook. Negro ministers or elevator boys or body servants are often included to furnish comic relief; they continue to add life and interest to scenes on Southern estates, or in Pullman cars, or at the race track, or in the great hotels. Without them American novelists and dramatists would often be hard put to it for comedy and an escape from routine or from tragic intensity.

To name the American novelists of the last forty years who have employed the negro character, in one way or another, is virtually to name all our novelists of that period. Harold Frederic, John Fox, Alice French, Maurice Thompson, Mary N. Murfree, Hamlin Garland, Owen Wister, Hopkinson Smith, to mention a few, have all followed in the footsteps of Simms, and made the negro either an amusing menial or else a stock figure useful in the action, or both.

---

14 *Harper's,* June, 1915.
15 *Collier's Weekly,* May, 1908.

Frank Stockton, Booth Tarkington, and others have shown some freshness of treatment, but the usual role of the negro has been slight. Although since Simms's day the current of American fiction has steadily shifted—first to a more polished romance, then to a mild realism, later still to a stern and uncompromising realism —and with it the conception of provincial peoples, yet except in novels of the last decade the negro has been unable to rise much beyond the position held in *The Yemassee* or *Swallow Barn*. Standards of accuracy established by Russell and Harris have of course affected longer works of fiction, so that the old coachman and voluble mammy of Miss Ellen Glasgow, for example, or of Miss Mary Johnston, are more lifelike than those of former periods; nevertheless the negro has usually lingered as a type too much taken for granted, and sketched according to the requirements of a well known conventionalism. Only in very recent years, with the change to decided realism, and an increased vogue for the problem novel, has this superficiality begun to give way.

The kinds of novel utilizing African characters have been many and varied, although most have in some way been concerned with the past. A case in point is the historical novel, such as Emerson Hough's *Purchase Price* (1910), or Winston Churchill's *Crisis* (1901), or almost any of Mary Johnston's volumes, or Ellen Glasgow's *Battle-Ground* (1902)—this last a study of Southern conditions after the Civil War, when the planter aristocracy and the new democracy were coming to blows. Romances of the Civil War, like Cyrus T. Brady's *Southerners* (1903); chronicles of reconstruction days, like Thomas Nelson Page's *Red Rock* (1898); belated answers to Mrs. Stowe, like Mrs. M. J. Bacon's *Lyddy* (1898); numerous volumes glorifying plantation society, like Robert A. Boit's *Eustace* (1884) or Mrs. Burton Harrison's *Flower de Hundred* (1890); melodramas on Southern life, like Elizabeth Merriweather's *Master of Red Leaf* (1880), Opie Read's *Kentucky Colonel* (1890), E. P. Roe's *Miss Lou* (1888), Thomas Dixon's *Leopard's Spots* (1902) and *The Clansman* (1905)—all afford place to the negro character, who is usually lifelike, but occasionally wooden, and in the melodramas, at least, sometimes reduced to the low estate of obsequious nonentity or brute. Many longer works of fiction have displayed, with success, the negro's humorous side, or his unusual psychology; Booth Tarkington's *Penrod and Sam* (1916) ex-

emplifies the first class, Frank Stockton's *Late Mrs. Null* (1886)
the second. Still other novels have treated the racial question, the
matter of mixed blood and white discrimination—best illustrated
in William Dean Howells's *An Imperative Duty* (1892), Gertrude
Atherton's *Senator North* (1900), and Dorothy Canfield Fisher's
Bent Twig (1915). Mrs. Fisher's book, which turns sharply away
from the conventional and smug handling of the negro, suggests
the work of a group of contemporary novelists, realists, and all with
a sociological bent. With them the novel on negro life enters a
new day.

Today the " negro question "—whatever can be said of the negro
character—is receiving widespread and vigorous discussion. Hardly
a year passes without the appearance of novels on miscegenation,
racial persecution, the need of the blacks to strike for a happier
position in American society. Into the books of even Southern
authors a new note has been entering. Mrs. Julia Peterkin's *Green
Thursday* (1924), a sympathetic and honest record of negro family
life in rural South Carolina, shows more openness of mind than
would have been likely twenty years ago; and so in a lesser degree
does *Porgy* (1925) by Dubose Heyward, the young Charleston poet.
A still stronger note of late, however, is that of protest, of rebel-
lion against the white man's smug civilization, rife with prejudices,
so critics contend, and cruelly oppressive towards all those not within
the pale. We have fallen upon the days of the problem novel; ours
is the heyday of the sociological propagandist, the student theorist,
who has naturally been attracted to the racial question.[16] Mary
White Ovington's *Shadow* (1920), T. S. Stribling's *Birthright*
(1922), Thompson-Hubbard's *Without Compromise* (1922), Clem-
ent Wood's *Nigger* (1922), H. A. Shands's *White and Black*

---

[16] How pressingly the negro has become a problem is at least suggested by
the number and quality of recent scholarly works on him. Aside from many
studies in *The Journal of Negro History*, and able researches by members of
the race like W. E. B. DuBois, Benjamin Brawley, Carter G. Woodson, Kelly
Miller, and T. W. Talley, the scholarly investigations by whites have of late
become increasingly serious. In 1924, for instance, W. D. Weatherford published his sociological treatise, *The Negro from Africa to America*; in 1925 the
University of North Carolina offered, through its press, *The Negro and His
Songs*, a compilation of source material for the study of folk-songs; and more
important than either, in 1920 appeared the first volume of Professor Leo
Wiener's work, *Africa and the Discovery of America*. Professor Wiener's
thesis—far-fetched no doubt, but showing the trend of the times—is that before
the days of Columbus, African navigators reached America, where they remained long enough to affect aboriginal life and culture.

(1922), Joan Sutherland's *Challenge* (1926), and Walter White's
Flight (1926) are conspicuous among many novels on the negro
question which have appeared within the last ten years.[17]   Considered from the standpoint of what their authors intended—the
condemnation of social injustice—they are successful, but rarely
do the characters in them appear alive or human.   The authors have
made convincing arguments at the expense of characterization and
lifelike scenes and situations.   One author at least, Irvin Cobb, conscious of what is happening, allows the hero of *J. Poindexter,
Colored* (1922) to say of himself, " I ain't no problem, I'se a pusson;
I craves to be so regarded."   Pity it is more negro characters nowadays are not thus regarded by their creators.   Usually these artificial heroes are simply walking arguments; as in the days of Abolitionism, they exemplify some theory or embody a proof of the white
man's errors.   In Walter White's *Flight,* for instance, the heroine,
Mimi Daquin, who flees from her people, "goes white," and marries into the " superior " race, only in the end to be drawn back into
the fold of the blacks, is little more than a symbol of one great incongruous element in American society, the white negro class; her
life and perplexities arouse the reader to a hatred of Nordic prejudices, yet Mimi herself is a puppet, scarcely human at all.   Nowise
better is Peter Siner, hero of T. S. Stribling's widely discussed
Birthright.   Mr. Stribling has made clear how hard is the lot of
the educated black below the Mason and Dixon's line, how narrow
his life, how cramped his outlook, how meager his opportunities
for culture, how stifling is the atmosphere of the black districts in
which he dwells, how often he is duped and preyed upon by white
neighbors; on the other hand the author fails to invest Peter with a
convincing reality which makes the reader expect, some day, to
meet him on the street.   To say that *Birthright* represents with
fair accuracy the level of our present day problem novels is to admit how, from the point of view of literary art, they all fail.   Their
negro characters occupy a different position—on the whole, a much
more important one—from that of the menials and humorous black
folk in the fiction of Miss Glasgow or Frank Stockton; but they do
not so much touch the imagination or the heart.   The newer atti-

---

17 With these compare Mrs. Sarah Gertrude Millin's *God's Stepchildren*
(1924), a story of miscegenation in Africa, and one of the strongest problem
novels of our day.   Mrs. Millin is an Englishwoman.

tude, however, is healthier, fuller of possibilities; it is much more likely than the old to lead eventually to a thoroughgoing comprehension of the African, and hence to penetrating portrayals of his inner self—of his ambitions, his emotions, his latent capacities.

III

With the American drama the story has been much the same as with the novel. Until recently no important play has employed the negro as protagonist. But American playwrights have, like our novelists, valued him as an entertaining and convenient figure for minor roles. Such were his parts in many plays on the Civil War—Elliot Barnes's *Blue and the Gray* (1884),[18] C. P. Dazey's *For a Brother's Life* (1885), William Gillette's *Held by the Enemy* (1886), Clyde Fitch's *Barbara Frietchie* (1899), James A. Herne's *Reverend Griffith Davenport* (1899); and in plantation melodramas, such as C. P. Dazey's *In Old Kentucky* (1882) and J. K. Tillotson's *Planter's Wife* (1883). In *May Blossom* (1884), David Belasco utilized the oft-repeated theme of slave loyalty; *The Beautiful Slave* (1891) and Lottie Parker's *Under Southern Skies* (1901) are concerned with another threadbare subject, race consciousness; and in *The Faith Healer* (1910), William Vaughan Moody made use of still a third, the African's religiousness, with its admixture of superstition. The minstrel tradition has continued, not only in the occasional performances of lingering minstrel troops, but in altered versions of *Uncle Tom's Cabin,* and in a large class of musical comedy—*A Girl from Dixie* (1903), for example—in which the negro element becomes at times the mainstay of the entertainment. In *The Nigger* (1909) of Edward Sheldon a step forward was made, although no great or startling one, for the playwright falls short not only in characterization but in the handling of a powerful situation: a proud Southerner's discovery that he is partly negro—a situation calling for the powers of a Hugo or a Shakespeare. Such powers Sheldon of course lacked, but his play succeeded on the stage, and— more important here—allotted to the negro a role conspicuous and important.

No more noteworthy use of the dramatic possibilities latent in the negro was made until 1921, when Eugene O'Neill wrote the most

---

[18] Unless otherwise indicated, the dates here given refer to the year of presentation on the stage.

sensational play of the year, *The Emperor Jones*. Although not altogether convincing in its characterization, *The Emperor Jones* powerfully exhibits certain qualities of the negro race seldom more than suggested: a cunning and half intuitive wisdom, a strain of weird superstition, a reverential and awed respect in the presence of great manifestations of nature, darkness, the mingled sounds of the night, the mysterious nocturnal appearance of the tropical forest, and to a certain extent a disdainful and antagonistic attitude toward the white man. In this play O'Neill was, one feels, manfully striving to get at the heart and soul of a people—to see if the laughable black folk so long taken for granted, and " read at a glance by every true Southerner," had not, after all, spiritual depths not yet sounded. His failure to make more of his subject is owing, not to any lack of intelligent effort or ability, but to the absence of long, first hand acquaintance with his subject. Other plays in the same general class with *The Emperor Jones*—Ridgely Torrence's *Granny Maumee*,[19] for example, or Paul Greene's *White Dresses*[20]—need hardly be reviewed. They all savor too much of the workshop; they show too much striving after elusive psychological effects, and too evident an attempt to give sociological data a local habitation if not a name. Upon reading such a play one feels that the author must have said, " Behold, I will write a play in which to exemplify my analysis of the African!" He failed to think in terms of flesh-and-blood character, of a human personality conceived, but personified racial traits and social phenomena. The recent realistic drama on the negro is suggestive, however, and *The Emperor Jones*,[21] at least, holds the promise of more commendable presentations of him yet to come.

IV

These more commendable presentations may perhaps be forthcoming from the negroes themselves, although to date the signs of such a happening are few. It is disappointing, in reviewing the record of authorship among American negroes, to find how few have produced poetry or fiction of more than ordinary worth. In the

---

[19] Published in New York, 1917.
[20] In B. R. Lewis's *Contemporary One-Act Plays*, New York, 1922.
[21] O'Neill's more recent play on the negro, *All God's Chillun Got Wings* (New York, 1924), fails dismally; it is strained, unnatural, not even entertaining.

fifties, when Abolitionism was raging, and Frederick Douglass, William Wells Brown, and others were selling their autobiographical volumes to enthusiastic Northern readers, the cry went up, "Give this people a chance, and they will produce their own Homers and Miltons and Shakespeares!" So far the optimism of that cry has not been justified. Perhaps the race has not yet had the chance; perhaps the period of development and education has been too brief. Whatever answer may be offered, the fact remains that few American negroes have been true makers of literature. When one has named Phillis Wheatley, Mrs. Frances E. W. Harper, Booker T. Washington, Paul Laurence Dunbar, William S. Braithwaite, A. A. Whitman, C. W. Chesnutt, W. E. B. DuBois, Benjamin Brawley, James Weldon Johnson, Claude McKay, Georgia Douglass Johnson, and Countee Cullen, the list is practically exhausted, and there are included names significant only in the light of history. From the group, DuBois and Dunbar stand out—the former for his prose, the latter for his poetry. No other book of the class has reached the high level of DuBois's *Darkwater* (1920), a defiant challenge to the white race, which moves by the audacity of its charges, and the denunciatory eloquence of its protest. No other negro has written so powerfully in prose. In poetry, the race has proved somewhat abler, for although Dunbar is preeminent among negro poets, he is only one of several of undeniable gift. Within a narrow range, and when he could leave off imitation, Dunbar proved himself a true singer. Some of his best lyrics, frequently in dialect, reflect the well known characteristics of his race—its happy abandon, its joy in the present moment, its keen delight in the senses, its spontaneity of word and act, and its occasional melancholy and wistfulness.

In prose fiction the American negro has accomplished little. The crude volumes of Mrs. Frances Harper and William Wells Brown represent the earliest attempts worth noticing, and since the Civil War few that are much superior have appeared. DuBois's one effort at fiction, *The Quest of the Silver Fleece* (1911), failed to bring him any vast glory. Dunbar's wife, Mrs. Alice Dunbar-Nelson, proved an apt imitator of Cable, but otherwise her work lacks distinction. Dunbar himself wrote both novels and short stories, but his prose at its best, as in *The Sport of the Gods* (1902), appears decidedly inferior to his poetry. *The Uncalled* (1896), his first novel, has some value as autobiography, and may possibly endure as an incidental record of the author's life, although certainly not as fiction proper.

Only one negro, in fact—Charles W. Chesnutt—can seriously lay claim to the title of novelist, and for the most part, Chesnutt was more propagandist than literary artist.   He dissipated his energies in working for the social betterment of his people—an effort natural enough, and laudable, but none the less damaging to his literary ventures.   Chesnutt's more successful works, such as *The Wife of His Youth*[22] and *The House Behind the Cedars* (1900), are not, it is to be feared, so typical of him as *The Marrow of Tradition* (1901), a bitter attack on the Southern whites.   The novel is unfair in tone, crudely partisan in design, inflammatory in suggestion, and worthless except as a polemical tract.   Southern whites, so the novelist contends, not only engage in mob riots, but enjoy them; when a negro is to be sacrificed to appease the sectional thirst for blood, the occasion is enthusiastically celebrated:

> Already the preparations were under way for the impending execution.   A T-rail from the railroad yard had been procured, and men were burying it in the square before the jail. Others were bringing chains, and a load of pine wood was piled in convenient proximity.   Some enterprising individual had begun the erection of seats from which, for a pecuniary consideration, the spectacle might be the more easily and comfortably viewed.
>
> Ellis was stopped once or twice by persons of his acquaintance.   From one he learned that the railroad would run excursions from the neighboring towns in order to bring spectators to the scene; from another that the burning was to take place early in the evening, so that the children might not be kept up beyond their usual bedtime.   In one group that he passed he heard several young men discussing the question of which portions of the negro's body they should prefer for souvenirs.[23]

Misrepresentations of this complexion must not only fail in winning support in a campaign, but much more in presenting a true picture of the people oppressed.   For lifelike characterizations of negroes one might as profitably turn to the volumes of infuriated Abolitionist novelists.

------

22 In *The Wife of His Youth, and Other Stories of the Color-Line,* Boston, 1899.
23 *The Marrow of Tradition,* 219-20.

Since Chesnutt's day the novel by negro authors has in nowise improved; it remains either an instrument for the spread of propaganda or else is puerile in execution—both of which shortcomings are illustrated in Jessie R. Fauset's *There Is Confusion* (1924). With poetry, however, the negro continues to have more success. During the past year few young poets have attracted as much attention as Countee Cullen. Whether negro dramatists and novelists can rise to the level of the poets, and by maintaining an impartial point of view, set forth their race accurately and with disinterested insight, yet remains to be seen.[24]

V

Whether any author, in fact, either white or black, can successfully portray the negro in the heavy roles of tragedy also remains to be seen. Some commentators contend that the true African—essentially gay, happy-go-lucky, rarely ambitious or idealistic, the eternal child of the present moment, able to leave trouble behind—is unsuited for such portrayal. Others have taken an opposite view. "Think," writes one, "of the negro of good education, artistic sensibilities, or high social purposes who never gets away from his origin, who meets galling rebuffs from the whites in all sections of the country, and is scorned and suspected by his own people! Possibility enough for tragedy there! Booker Washington without his poise and persistent optimism would have been the protagonist of a tragedy unspeakable. . . . Is it not a mere question of time until a tragedy thus inherent and inevitable shall find expression through some one with insight to read it truly and with genius to set it forth artistically?"[25] Even more outspoken are several negro critics, who denounce the conception of Uncle Remus as outworn and childish and call insistently for newer treatments, fresh, more dignified, epic in scope. One of these critics, Mr. Benjamin Brawley, declares: "The Negro himself as the irony of American civilization is the supreme challenge to American literature. Like Banquo's ghost he will not down. All faith and hope, all love and longing,

---

[24] For further information on authorship among negroes, see Benjamin Brawley: *The Negro in Literature and Art,* New York, 1918; and the pamphlet by Robert T. Kerlin, *Contemporary Poetry of the Negro,* Hampton, Va., 1921. See also *The New Negro: An Interpretation* (edited by Alain Locke), New York, 1925.

[25] *The Dial,* June 8, 1916.

all rapture and despair, look out from the eyes of this man who is ever with us and whom we never understand.   Gentle as a child, he has also the strength of Hercules.   The more we think we know him the more unfathomable he is."[26]   Perhaps agreement on what is possible with the negro in fiction is, as on most other human questions, to be sought in vain; and certainly speculations are futile when the subject is a whole race, embracing millions of individuals widely different in conformity to type, in capacity, and in this instance, in purity of blood.   The wiser course is to weigh carefully the facts of performance.

If we take the high standard of Aristotelian tragedy, and hold that success with characters means portrayal on the epic scale of Oedipus and Lear and Hester Prynne, then the admission must follow that American authors have failed with the negro type.   But if the somewhat less lofty standard of comedy be deemed sufficient —if to succeed may mean setting forth, with sympathy and insight, the human attributes, even the laughable frailties, of humbler heroes —the verdict, surely, must be reversed.   Only the mulatto and others of mixed blood have, so far, furnished us with material for convincing tragedy.   The pure black has been, at best, only wistful or mildly pathetic; usually he has appeared amusing even in his ambitions and strivings; nearly always he provokes a laugh or at least a smile.   Thousands of readers of American literature have been entertained by his drollery, his incongruous display of civilization and savagery, his poetical outlook on the world.   Without exemplifying exalted qualities or filling the position of epic hero, he has proved a great comic type, and for many decades has lent to much of American fiction a raciness, an enlivening element, a savor of the natural and primitive which could ill be spared.

---

[26] *The Bookman,* October, 1922.

INDEX